Big Eyes

BIG EYES

The Southwestern Photographs of
Simeon Schwemberger, 1902–1908

Paul V. Long

Essay by Michele M. Penhall

University of New Mexico Press
Albuquerque

Library of Congress Cataloging-in-Publication Data

Long, Paul V., 1933–

Big Eyes : the Southwestern photographs of Simeon Schwemberger,

1902–1908 / Paul V. Long ; essay by Michele M. Penhall. — 1st ed.

p.   cm.

Includes bibliographical references.

ISBN 0-8263-1302-7

1. Navajo Indians—Pictorial works.   2. Pueblo Indians—Pictorial

works.   3. Schwemberger, Simeon.   4. Photographers—Southwest, New—

Biography.   5. Franciscans—Southwest, New—Biography.

I. Schwemberger, Simeon.   II. Penhall, Michele M.   III. Title.

E99.N3L76   1992

979'.031'0222—dc20   *91-24923*

CIP

FRONTISPIECE: *Dine Tsosi, Slim Navajo, last of the Navajo war chiefs, 1906.*

CONTENTS

ACKNOWLEDGMENTS

In any endeavor, there are many whose names do not appear on the title page. If it were not for these dedicated and understanding people, no research project would achieve its goal of publication. It is fitting, then, that those who have made possible this work be given recognition for their many hours of assistance in identifying photographs and giving suggestions, advice, and encouragement.

Foremost is the late Dr. Leland Wyman whose eclectic interest uncovered a large collection of valuable historical material stored in the Franciscan Mission at St. Michaels, Arizona. During the summer of 1963, while carrying on research on the Navajo reservation, he was requested by the Franciscan Fathers to help them find someone who would be able to make order out of an estimated 2,000 glass-plate negatives dating from about 1902 to 1908, which were in their possession. Nearly 400 of the negatives were produced by Brother Simeon Schwemberger, who had been assigned to St. Michaels Mission in 1901.

This request was forwarded to Dr. Edward B. Danson, the director of the Museum of Northern Arizona in Flagstaff. His interest and excitement over the possibilities of the historic collection were infectious. As curator of photography at the Museum of Northern Arizona, I was informed about the collection at St. Michaels in several brief meetings with Dr. Danson and quickly began to see its historic value. The early correspondence with Father Emanuel Trockur of the Franciscans intensified my interest in the project as he briefly summarized the subject matter of the glass plates. The more I learned of their content the more interesting they became. I was excited at the prospect not only of seeing this massive collection but also of having the privilege of making prints from the negatives. During the following months I prodded Dr. Danson to find the necessary funds to do at least a cursory study of the collection.

In 1967 he found funds through the museum's research monies. At the same time he secured additional financing through the generosity of Dr. C. Gregory Crampton of the Western History Center of the University of Utah. These funds were used during the summer of 1967 to clean, print, and identify the glass-plate negatives.

In addition, Dr. Bernard L. Fontana was instrumental in obtaining another grant from the Doris Duke Foundation for the printing and cataloging of 3,500 film negatives also in the St. Michaels archives.

The fathers of the Order of Friars Minors (O.F.M.), notably Fathers Davin Von Hagel, Marcon Hetterberg, Celestine Bauman, and Kristin Hocker, opened their doors and their hearts to the project, giving time and enthusiasm to every stage of the lengthy process of cleaning, printing, and cataloging the glass plates. They provided their friendship and their interest and made the time away from home and family pass quickly. Gratitude does not seem to be enough for their service. Much credit is due the brothers of the order who, each in his own way, made my stay at St. Michaels enjoyable: Peter, Mark, Matthew, Timothy, Donald, and Gregory.

I want especially to recognize the late Father Emanuel Trockur, O.F.M., then the oldest living Franciscan on the Navajo reservation, who gave freely of his time and his encyclopedic knowledge of people and places so that the photographs could be identified and the project completed quickly and efficiently. His wit and sense of humor made each day brighter than the day before.

Despite his many duties at St. Michaels School, Father John Lanzrath, O.F.M., spent many hours in the identification of people and places. Even after the project ended, Father John continued his efforts to find people who might know the faces and places portrayed on the glass plates. In this way he contributed a number of identifications to previously unidentified photographs.

Among the Navajos who were instrumental in identification and in providing insight into Simeon Schwemberger's character, two are outstanding: Bernadine Whitegoat and John Watchman.

Lucy Nez and Angie Hubbell worked at the exacting task of cataloging and filing the completed prints.

Over the years Martin Link and David Brugge have maintained a constant watch for additional photographs credited to Simeon Schwemberger and for information on his missionary and postmissionary activities in the Gallup area. Both have provided valuable assistance in the compilation of data for this book. In addition, the hospitable Martin Link provided bed and breakfast for those times when I had to be in Gallup. The late evening conversations with Link added greatly to my understanding of the function of the brothers of the Order of Friars Minors.

Mike Andrews, former curator of the St. Michaels Historical Museum, and his gracious wife, Judy, were of inestimable help. Mike's encouragment, knowledge of mission history, and rapport with the Franciscans were instrumental in securing permission to reproduce the photographs included in this book. It was also through him that I received permission to use the St. Michaels darkroom to print the glass plates, which make up the bulk of the illustrations.

Octavia Fellin, former librarian of the Gallup Public Library, provided encouragement and hard-to-find resources concerning Schwemberger. Throughout the research she was always available for consultation and suggestions.

Eunice Fellin, daughter of Simeon Schwemberger, graciously consented to several interviews. Her remembrances of her father's Gallup trading post, and the physical arrangements and the activities that went on at the post have given me greater insight into Simeons's character and talents. She also provided a photograph of Simeon and a snapshot of the old trading post.

Nello Guadagnoli, owner of fifty of Schwemberger's glass plates, gave permission to view the prints in his collection.

Diana Fane, curator of the Department of African, Oceanic, and North American Art at the Brooklyn Museum, and Lise Michaelman, anthropologist of the same institution, provided numerous references and photographs from the field reports and journals of Stewart Culin.

I am indebted to Dr. James C. Faris of the University of Connecticut for his suggestions and information on the Nightway. It was through his research that the singer for the 1905 Nightway ceremony was identified. He also aided in the correct captioning of the Nightway photographs which appear in this book.

John Havens, the son of the late Peter Havens, was most helpful in locating the only photographs that his father had that were taken by Schwemberger.

Much support during the writing and preparation of this book was provided by Barton Wright, a long-time friend and companion from our early days at the Museum of Northern Arizona. I greatly appreciate his help, faith, and encouragement. His positive attitude has helped me over many rocks and shoals.

I would also like to thank all those who read and critiqued the various drafts of the manuscript: L. P. "Pick" Temple, Barton Wright, and David Brugge. Their corrections have been incorporated and many of their recommendations have been followed; any remaining errors are mine. I am also grateful to my editor, Dana Asbury, for her patience and encouragement. The enthusiasm of Beth Hadas is also most sincerely appreciated.

And finally, my family has supported this endeavor from its inception. To them I am indebted for their encouragement and love through this project.

PREFACE

Toward the end of the summer of 1963, the late Dr. Leland Wyman informed the Museum of Northern Arizona of the existence of a large collection of glass-plate negatives stored at the Franciscan Mission house at St. Michaels, Arizona, on the Navajo reservation a short distance west of Window Rock, the capitol of the Navajo Nation. Furthermore, the Franciscans made a request that someone be found who would be interested in the collection. Fathers Emanuel Trockur and John Lanzrath wished that the body of the photographs be put into usable order and preserved so that they could form the basis of a Franciscan archive at St. Michaels.

It was the following August before I was able to visit the mission and make a cursory study of the photographic archives. This preliminary investigation revealed nearly 2,000 glass-plate negatives stored in the basement of the mission in apple crates and cardboard cartons and on open shelves.

I had only a short time for this initial work, but as each succeeding negative was cleaned it became apparent that this collection was outstanding not only in its subject matter but also in the quality of the photography.

In addition to the glass-plates negatives, 3,000 film negatives were in storage at the mission. A number of these negatives are on nitrate-base films. Yet, it took three years to obtain funds to proceed adequately with the task of cleaning, printing, identifying, and cataloging the large collection. Once the funds became available I went to St. Michaels and began the two-month-long project.

The process of cleaning the glass plates required the utmost care since many of the negatives already exhibited pressure cracks from their long, inadequate storage. The base side of each plate, the shiny side, was cleaned with water and a soft cloth. The emulsion side was lightly dusted with a camel's hair brush and with light air pressure. Fortunately, the accumulated dust and grime were removed in this manner with unexpected ease.

The photographs that appear in this book were made by contact printing. Over the years, fungus had begun to develop on many of the plates, making them difficult to print. There were some from which a reproducible print was impossible to obtain.

Once cleaning and preparing the plates was concluded this material became a part of the mission archive, adding immensely to the early history of the mission and to the visual record early Navajo life.

Prints are on file in the repositories of both the Museum of Northern Arizona and the archive at St. Michaels. Once the print were made, identification of the subjects of the photographs required months and, in some cases, years. Days of looking at prints and asking questions of Father Emanuel Trockur resulted in the identification of many of the sixty-year-old photographs. Occasionally, Father Emanuel was unable to identify the people and could only guess at their names. Fortunately, his memory was excellent, and by double checking with older Navajos, the identities were substantiated.

Twenty-eight years have passed since the salvage project was begun, and in this time many have sought the Schwemberger photographs, with monetary gain often being the motivating factor. The fathers, however, have remained steadfast in their desire keep these negative preserved and at the mission.

Over the years more facts have been uncovered concerning Simeon Schwemberger. It is fortunate that the present book was not completed in the sixties; in 1988, new information led to the discovery of a series of journals kept by Stewart Culin, an anthropologist who spent summers between 1904 and 1911 on the Navajo reservation. His journals and his field notes were illustrated with Simeon Schwemberger's photographs. His journals referred to Simeon numerous times, as they were good friends. Much of the information from these journal entries substantiates what had been gleaned from Schwemberger's personal letters. They have all been instrumental in revealing the personality and temperament of Schwemberger.

Because of the timing of the initial study, a number of elderly Navajo informants were available for interviewing. All of them have since died.

Despite the conditions under which the Schwemberger plates were stored, the majority of them were printable and produced quite acceptable prints. The opportunity to work with this valuable collection of Simeon Schwemberger's photographs has given me insight into the early years of the twentieth century, a period that has always been of deep interest to me.

Big Eyes

1. Simeon Schwemberger with his camera, 1907.

INTRODUCTION

The great majority of early photographs of the West were taken by men who were, by the standards of the day, professionals. Photography satisfied their desire to record the world around them.

Unlike those nineteenth-century men who photographed the Southwest as a professional vocation, the Franciscan missionaries of St. Michaels Mission on the Navajo reservation were missionaries first and recorders of the human activities about them second. To Brother Simeon Schwemberger and Fathers Egbert Fisher and Emanuel Trockur, photography was an avocation. As servants of God their primary purpose was to bring Christianity to the people.

That they were able to make these photographs over the years can be attributed to their training and perseverance. Their photographs portray the Native American as a dignified individual. Evidence of their contact with European culture is not apparent, with the exception of their Western clothing and the wagons and cars that have been added to their cultural inventory. The transition from a native religious system to one introduced by the Catholic missionaries is apparent in the many school and confirmation photographs

3

in the collection. It is plain to see from these images that the Franciscan Fathers loved these people to whom they had been sent to spread the word of God. They not only were interested in missionary work but also were instrumental in gaining a political platform for the Navajo to expand their reservation and acquire territories that were traditionally within their pre-Conquest boundaries. It was through Anselm Weber, O.F.M., that the Navajo reservation boundaries were expanded during the late 1800s and early 1900s for the primary purpose of providing more grazing land for the expanding flocks of sheep owned by the "People." He worked tirelessly on behalf of the Navajo by promoting tribal ownership and arguing against family allotments on reservation land. He plainly saw that it would be impossible to establish a new religion in the area without first gaining the Navajos' confidence. It is a paradox to some that by this attitude and understanding he provided the "People" with the strength to prevent cultural breakdown.[1]

Weber's involvement with the Navajo on every level was matched by all the subsequent missionaries who worked with the Navajo. In a small way Weber understood the concept of culture change (acculturation). One tactic the missionaries used was to identify those things that the native people were proud of and then make complimentary statements about them. The recipients of the compliments thereby gained confidence and were more receptive to new thoughts and ideas. This was a long-range endeavor, and Weber was willing to do what he could during his time as a missionary to bring about the change that he was sure would come.[2]

The purpose of this book is not to review the history of the Catholic church in Arizona and New Mexico. However, it is worthwhile to discuss briefly the Catholic mission philosophy and how the Franciscan Fathers of St. Michaels interpreted it and brought it to bear on some of the problems that confronted them in the Navajo country.

This approach to native peoples had been developed, tried, and proven successful among the people of both Central and South America. The process of "reduction" required that the native people be gathered into pueblos or towns. Once they were established in communities conversion could occur more easily, especially with the children, through schools and church functions. The mission building was to be the central core of such a village.

Early eighteenth-century missionary attempts resulted in some conversions, especially of children, but only because the missionaries promised the Navajo "mares, mules, horses, cows, clothing, and many sheep."[3]

As for the adult Navajo, the majority were not interested in embracing the Catholic church. Several factors signify the failure of early attempts to bring the Navajos into the "fold." Primarily, they were not interested in living in villages, preferring instead to wander unattached. Secondly, the Navajo allowed the white missionaries to be in their country only as long as they brought gifts. Finally, the Navajo did not allow their children to be taken by the strangers for religious indoctrination.[4]

Despite early failures the Franciscans arrived to establish a mission and school in October 1898. Brother Placid was, at forty-six years, the oldest in the new community. Father Juvenal Schnorbus and Father Anselm Weber were ten years younger.

Apparently, the experiences of the early missionaries had reached the Franciscans in Cincinnati, Ohio, for one of the first things that Father Anselm did before their departure to Arizona was to write Dr. Washington Matthews, a well-known anthropologist who had studied the Navajo, for information about them. Father Anselm was supplied with all of Matthews's current publications and with valuable advice. Matthews recommended that the missionaries immediately develop a vocabulary of their own. Shortly before the fathers left for Arizona, Matthews reinforced his procedure for missionary work. "My opinion is that if you want to reach the *hearts* of the people and gain a permanent influence over them, you cannot too soon begin to learn the Navajo language."[5]

The Franciscans' desire to learn the language required that they spend as much time as possible with the Navajo; thus the "coffee pot was always on" in the small kitchen of the mission. As Father Weber met more Navajos, he took every opportunity to learn new words and to write down new expressions. Eventually, the three Franciscans were no longer being laughed at as they read back their new words to the Navajos.

With their rudimentary vocabulary growing and their pronunciation improving the friars began to seek a means to carry out their mission at St. Michaels. They decided to begin a school for a few Navajo boarding pupils with the hope of expanding it. The primary responsibility for teaching rested with the fathers. The brothers of the Order of Friars Minors performed the arduous tasks around the mission home. They built buildings, planted and tended the gardens, dug wells, and fed the residents. Later, electrical systems and a telephone line were needed. While the brothers had some basic training in religions, philosophy, and Latin, most of their education had been in the trades, especially carpentry, farming, and electricity. It was their responsibility to care for the physical aspect of the mission while the fathers tended to the spiritual needs of the Indians as well as of the Franciscan community.

THE LIFE OF SIMEON SCHWEMBERGER

The Early Years

George Charles Schwemberger was born in Cincinnati, Ohio, on August 16, 1867. He was baptized on September 12, 1867, in the St. Francis Parish church. His early education probably consisted of classes at a parochial elementary school where he learned his catechism along with the normal curriculum. He was confirmed on August 11, 1883, in St. George's Church in Corryville, Ohio, at the age of sixteen. He attended a minor seminary for high–school–age youth. He was apparently bright, and that he did not enter the seminary as a candidate for the priesthood is difficult to explain. He probably did not have the personality that the superiors desired in a priest, so he was accepted as a brother.

His initial step toward service to his church was not a difficult decision. In the summer of 1887, when he was twenty, he became a candidate for the religious Order of Friars Minor, the Franciscans. The primary focus of the Franciscan brothers was in the trades. The brothers of the Order of Friars Minor were responsible for the everyday operation of this mission homes. Every chore, no matter how big or small, fell to the brothers of the order. Unlike the fathers, who had a strict,

7

2. Simeon Schwemberger at work in the mission garden, 1905. Photographer unknown, but perhaps Elizabeth Funk took this photograph since she was cooking at the mission for a short time.

structured curriculum of study for the priesthood, the broth-ers were immediately put to work in various tasks of manual labor, even if they were not trained for the job. A brother was often assigned to work in areas that were totally alien to his experience. On many occasions these duties were so irksome that the brother exhibited extreme stress. Schwemberger was just such an example. Although he was adept at mechanical activities, he did not enjoy domestic chores, which included cooking and shopping for the house commissary. This stress eventually led to difficulties with the superior. After all, a brother's duty was to do whatever job he was assigned, obediently, without comment. Schwemberger's personality did not allow for total subservience, a characteristic that was almost demanded for by the system of that time. To balk at this structure was to court disaster in personal relationships, especially in a small, confined, and isolated religious community. His real love was working outdoors with the vegetable and flower gardens. Apparently his talents lay in his ability to fix things, talents that would serve him well in the years to come.

In 1896 Schwemberger received four votes out of four in favor of his taking his solemn vows. Probably at this time he was given his clerical name, Simeon. Little information concerning the activities of Schwemberger from 1896 to 1901 is available. He was probably assigned to a parish church for at least four or five years before he requested the Indian mission field. His request was honored during the summer of 1901. He was assigned to the Navajo mission field, replacing Brother Placid, one of the original Franciscans who established the St. Michaels mission church in 1898. Sometime during the summer of 1901 Brother Simeon boarded the train in Cincinnati for the West.

The five years that the Franciscans had been at St. Michaels had been fruitful years. They had developed written vocabulary and pronunciation of the Navajo language. Positive steps had been taken with the various Navajo leaders toward establishing a school at St. Michaels. Only a few months after Brother Simeon's arrival actual planning for a school began, and on November 1, 1901, bids were opened for the construction of St. Michaels school.[1] J. H. Owen of Minneapolis won the bid. Construction began in March of 1902. Owen's workers, supplemented by Indian laborers, pushed the work along rapidly. It was several weeks before the Owen Construction group was able to erect it's own "mess house" and during that time Brother Simeon cooked for all the construction workers, in addition to the Franciscans.[2]

Simeon did not sleep in the house, but in a room in an empty house about three-quarters of a mile away "to keep unwanted guests from the property."[3]

In the summer of 1902 Mother Katherine Drexel made a tour of the area and, fortunately, her traveling companion, Sister Ignatius, was a keen observer. Sister Ignatius's detailed observations give a good description of Simeon's appearance as well as his personality: " . . . A good hearted brother (Simeon Schwemberger, O.F.M.) who is chief cook, singer in the choir, head housekeeper and farmer, poultry raiser, laundry man, baker, altar server, etc., and generally useful everywhere appeared with sleeves rolled up disclosing a brawny arm, strong and well developed for frequent service in the Master's service."[4] He was a hearty and cheerful brother, according to Sister Ignatius, with a tendency for joking and teasing anyone who was within earshot.

Brother Schwemberger's cooking seems to have been palatable, at best. Sister Ignatius observed that the floor beneath the stove bore evidence of his frequent use of the frying pan, as it was covered with grease. Regardless, Sister Ignatius thought of him as the "best-hearted" person she had ever seen. His laugh was frequently heard throughout the one-story house. Apparently he was not a quiet person, and, given Weber's own pious personality it is obvious that Simeon was not quite what Weber felt a Franciscan should be.

Simeon told the sister that he remained quiet only when the Father Provincial and the sisters were around. The Father Provincial visited only once a year.[5] Schwemberger also informed the sister that a few months after he arrived at the mission, the superior, Anselm Weber, told him he was only half civilized and so he believed it.[6] He commented to the sister that it was a good thing that he was out in the country where he could, as he expressed it, "holler and yell to his heart's content."[7]

Not all of Schwemberger's time was spent housekeeping and cooking. On December 5, 1902, Father Anselm and Frank Walker, mission interpreter, accompanied by Schwemberger, took the sister's team of heavy mules and a freight wagon to collect pupils for the school. Their first stop, just before nightfall, was at Silversmith's hogan. His hogan was one of the modern type. It had a door and a lock. Brother Simeon had to crawl through the smoke hole in order to unscrew the lock from the inside. The following day the group traveled to Charley Mitchell's and found his wife quite ill with a high fever. Simeon, who carried quinine with him at all times, administered the medicine to her. Despite the fact that her fever lowered, Charley and Silversmith, Charley's brother, agreed with the star-gazer that she had been "bewitched by a magic shots in the breast and neck by splinters of fang and antler." Silversmith rode ninety miles over the mountains to hire a medicine man.[8]

Weber, Walker, and Schwemberger returned about December 10 with nine children bundled up in the wagon. As far as I can determine this was the only time Brother Simeon accompanied Father Weber. Presumably, his housekeeping chores at the mission and the building of the school precluded any further excursions at that time.

By the end of 1905 there were three fathers to cook for and generally look after. Plans were also being laid for a new mission building, which would require brother Simeon's labors in various aspects. Although the actual building was contracted, Brother Simeon undoubtedly was pressed into service in those areas where he was most valuable—the digging and maintenance of the well and stringing the telephone line from the school to the new mission house.

For the next several years Simeon was busy with his housekeeping chores, cooking, the garden, and the well house. However as early as 1902 the financial records of the mission indicate that Schwemberger was involved in a small way with photography. From July to September there were monthly expenditures for photographic materials.[9] It was probably at this time that Brother Simeon entered into a written contract with the Franciscan superior, Father Weber, stating that he

3. Stewart Culin, anthropologist.
(Hereafter, titles in italics are Schwemberger's; additional explana-
tory caption notes are by Paul Long.) Culin spent several summers
in the area doing research first for the University of Pennsylvania
and later the Brooklyn Museum. A number of the photographs
used in this book were obtained from his field books.

would not seek payment of this work while a member of the Order of Friars Minor. At the same time Father Weber encouraged his work in photography, no doubt seeing its value as a historical record of the early mission. With Father Weber's blessings the mission fund purchased the camera and film for Simeon's photographic pursuit.[10]

Photographically, Schwemberger's most productive years, as evidenced from the house financial record, were 1904 through 1907.[11] Entries for 1906 are limited as far as expenses and income are concerned, and during 1908 and 1909 there are only three entries. However, Professor Stewart Culin's field notes for 1906 and 1907 contain many of Schwemberger's photographs of Old Oraibi following the discontent between the "Friendlies" and "Hostiles." Thus, Simeon was actively engaged in photography during 1906, at least as much as he could be with his other duties at the mission. In February 1906, he wrote Culin that "if I had the time I am sure I could sell several hundred dollars worth [of photographs] without any great effort but as it is I have absolutely no time to devote to photography. I am alone to do the work, not only cook and housekeeper but the other chores besides and pump house, etc."[12]

By April of that year Brother Simeon wrote to J. L. Hubbell (John Lorenzo Hubbell) that he had been working in the garden for two weeks and that "Manning's celebrated cook" was doing the housework.[13]

As early as 1904 Father Weber wrote to the Father Provincial making it quite clear that Brother Simeon did not like doing the housework. However, as Weber stated, he was in his element and working "very faithfully" outside of the kitchen, putting in water systems and plumbing the inside and the outside of the mission house. In addition to these tasks he was putting up telephone poles and stringing wire between the school, store, and mission building. Father Weber was very pleased with his work and commented that he

4. Bonina, the cook at St. Michaels mission, ca. 1906.

had certainly saved several hundred dollars in doing the work himself. The superior was concerned, however, that he had to hire Indian cooks while Simeon was working outside. But Weber conceded that cooks were cheaper than plumbers. Father Anselm wished that he could do his outside work as well as his housekeeping. It is evident from this correspondence that when Schwemberger was responsible for the cooking and housekeeping he always came up short of the expectations of his superior. At this time Simeon was also having misgivings about his role as a Franciscan, for the letter indicates that Simeon had mentioned that he might ask to be excused from the order just before the summer chapter.[14]

For some unknown reason, according to Father Weber's comments to the Father Provincial, Simeon was not liked by anyone in the house, although Father Weber had no serious complaints about him as long as he was willing to do the type of handyman work that he had been doing in 1904.[15] Perhaps the food being served in the house was not as good as it could have been. Dissatisfaction with the cooking certainly would strain any kind of personal relations that might have developed between Simeon and the fathers. That, coupled with Simeon's rather boisterous demeanor and his dislike for housekeeping chores, may have been unsettling for the more pious fathers.[16]

Certainly, the stress and pressure of nonacceptance were growing. Brother Simeon's response was to immerse himself more fully in his photography, when the time permitted. In 1905 Schwemberger produced many important photographs of the Navajo and Rio Grande Pueblo people and ceremonies. In late 1905 he photographed the Yeibichai (Nightway) series, one of his most important contributions to the photographic history of the Navajo (see pages 39–75).

The ceremony traditionally lasts nine day, but this particular one was interrupted due to the patient's wife beginning her menstrual cycle. Consequently, a period of fourteen days was required for the ceremony to be completed. The ceremony was halted from November 5 to November 10, when it was restarted, ending on November 15.[17]

Even in the early years of the century the Navajos were not easily persuaded to give permission to photograph such sacred ceremonies. It took Simeon much time and money to gain the permission of the medicine man and his patient to be photographed.[18] A thorough explanation of the steps taken to gain Schwemberger's participation in this event appears in the following section in his own words.

By 1905 Brother Schwemberger must have had a much better relationship with Father Anselm to be allowed to spend the time needed to photograph the Yeibichai ceremony in its entirety. It is also possible that Father Weber saw in Simeon's attendance the chance for greater rapport with the Navajo, for certainly copies of these photographs were given to the key participants. It was also a coup for Schwemberger. In the *McKinley County Republican* of December 9, 1905, an article appeared commenting in glowing terms about the series of "valuable" photographs taken by Brother Simeon. This notice would have helped him with sales had he had the time to produce photographs in any quantity, for they were an extraordinary collection of the activities of a Navajo sacred ceremony. It must have been gratifying to know that at last his photography was appreciated by the public.

During the same year, Brother Simeon made a trip to Cochiti and photographed a large number of people and some ceremonies for which each of the subjects was to receive a copy. His work around the mission had become so time-consuming that he had been unable to develop the plates and get the copies to the people who were writing to him in February 1906 asking where their pictures were. Schwemberger was discouraged and sorry that he could not get the prints made. He indicated that if he didn't get some help around the mission he would have to give up his photography which "gives me the blues."[19] Early in his mission days Brother Schwemberger had acquired a nickname which he seemed to prefer, since all of his correspondence was signed *Sim* or just *S.* Apparently he was also given a Navajo name— 'Anáá'tsoh, meaning "big eyes" or "bulging eyes."

Between 1904 and 1907, sales from Brother Schwemberger's photography were good. In fact, in 1906 and 1907, he managed to make a small profit for the Franciscans.

Little is known of Schwemberger during late 1907 and 1908. He is not heard from again until June 17, 1909. Stewart Culin's expedition report notes that Brother Simeon had left St. Michaels and the order to set up a photographic business in Gallup. The reason Culin gives for his departing the Franciscans was his infatuation with a young woman who had come to cook for the mission. Unfortunately, Brother Simeon had become involved. Apparently, the infatuation was one-sided, but he followed her to Gallup where she had gone to evade his unwanted advances. His mistake was in picking the sister of the husband of Father Weber's cousin upon whom to shower his affection. In quitting the mission he took the camera and glass plates, all property of the Franciscans.

The order showed him great consideration and made an effort to get dispensation from Rome to allow him to return to secular life and eventually to marry. There is no record that this dispensation was granted. In the meantime the girl became engaged to another man, thus leaving the unfortunate Schwemberger to face secular life alone. His knowledge of the world was limited since had led a cloistered existence for most of his life.[20]

Schwemberger was serious about his photography as a profession.
Probably in late 1909 Sim, as most of his friends called him,
opened his business in Gallup. His stationery gives no address
but proclaims his operation as the "Indian Arts Studio, Simeon Schwemberger, photographer." Across the top of the
page were the words "Photographers of the Navajo, and
Pueblo Indians, Landscapes, Prehistoric ruins, etc." Besides
photography, according to his letterhead, he had an interest in
Navajo blankets and silverware. Apparently, Schwemberger
sold Navajo crafts as well as operating a photography studio.

Schwemberger's activities as the proprietor of the Indian
Art Studio in Gallup are not documented. However, bits and
pieces of information from divergent sources have emerged
which may shed some light on his photographic pursuits.

In various archival collections, most notably the Hubbell
Trading Post National Monument, the Museum of Northern
Arizona, and Sharlot Hall Museum, photographic albums
and postcards that he produced have been preserved.

Schwemberger refers to three photographic albums in his
correspondence with Sharlot Hall. These albums were probably purchased from him during Hall's visit to Gallup in 1910.
Each album contained six pages bound by a heavy black
paper cover on which was imprinted, in white ink, the word
Photographs in script type. Ten five-by-seven-inch brown-
toned black-and-white photographs are bound in each volume. One album contains four separate photographs adhered
to three pages, apparently removed from a fourth album no
longer in existence.

Thirty-two of the photographs are of the Nightway ceremony. The remaining two are of Navajo chiefs Chee Dodge,
and Black Horse, and Tayoni together. It is possible that the
latter were taken at the 1905 Nightway.

Two similar albums are stored at Hubbell Trading Post National Monument. Both include photographs of the Nightway. One also has a few portraits of Navajo Indians and a number of photographs taken at Cochiti. In the other one are some scenic views and a few images of Hopi. Still another album ended up in the San Diego Museum of Man; it also contains the Nightway sequence. Schwemberger was obviously producing albums of his photographs, in his Gallup Studio, soon after he left the Franciscan mission at St. Michaels, early in 1909. How many albums were produced is unknown.

In addition to marketing photographic albums, Schwemberger ventured into the popular postcard business. Two collections of his postcards have been found, one at Hubbell Trading Post and the other at the Museum of Northern Arizona. The latter is by far the largest collection, consisting of seventy-three different views. The collection is further enhanced by the multiple copies of many of the postcards. Called *real* or *actual* photo postcards by collectors, they were extremely popular in the United States between 1900 and 1910.

Several of the postcards were mailed to Mrs. S. E. Day and carry dates ranging from August 18, 1908, to March 1910. Other cards dated May 12, 1909, in Schwemberger's handwriting were probably hand-delivered to Mrs. Day since on the address portion of the card are the initials A.B.D., presumably standing for Anna Burbridge Day, the wife of Sam E. Day. The earlier date, August 1908, helps to establish the beginning of the postcard production enterprise. It is possible that Schwemberger had left the mission as early as the fall of 1908 rather than in 1909 when Culin found out about his departure. The majority of the cards were postmarked in 1909. Sim was probably a full-time photographer and heavily involved with the distribution of postcards by late 1908 or early 1909.

5. Interior of John B. Moore's Crystal Trading Post, Crystal, New Mexico, c. 1906.

Besides the albums and postcards, Sim was engaged, in a minor way, with general commercial photography. The publishing of John P. Moore's Navajo rug catalog in 1911 gave Sim an outlet for his early photographs. Most were taken in 1906, probably at the suggestion of Moore, an opportunistic Indian trader who owned the Crystal Trading Post. Moore eventually produced three catalogs, between 1903 and 1911, dealing with Indian crafts. It is possible that the illustrations in the earlier two catalogs are also by Schwemberger.

The 1911 catalog, the last of the three published, was illustrated with seventeen black-and-white photographs and thirteen color plates. As color film was not available until twenty years later, it is assumed that the color plates, all of Navajo rugs, were produced in monochrome and, through lithography, reproduced in color.

All of the black-and-white photographs are credited to Simeon Schwemberger, and he probably made the rug photographs too. He may have initiated this project shortly after leaving the Franciscans; several of the black-and-white photographs included in the catalog are copyrighted 1906, so they must have come from this stock collection of negatives. Not all of the negatives from which the catalog photographs were reproduced have been located. The missing negatives include all of the rugs. Two negatives of rugs exist in the Museum of Northern Arizona collection, but they are not the ones that were published in the catalog.

In addition to having photographs published in the *McKinley County Republican* from time to time, Sim was commissioned to photograph buildings on the main street of Gallup (see Figs. 6 and 7). Not until he became a trader did his financial fortunes improve. What he earned as a photographer was minimal.

The Florida Connection

Sometime around December 1911 Simeon abandoned his photography business and worked for a short time for J. L. Hubbell at one of his trading posts. This employment was interrupted by an invitation from William Schwemberger, his younger brother, to come to Florida and join him in developing a winter resort. For a number of years William had been involved in the development and operation of a very successful summer resort in Brooksville, Indiana. Now he was planning to establish a winter vacation camp in Florida. Sim left Arizona at the end of January and busied himself in Florida with improvements around the property known as Camp Wil-

6. Caledonian Coal Company Building, Gallup, New Mexico, ca. 1908.

lard.[1] He was particularly interested in the agricultural poten-
tial of the area and soon had several acres cleared for grapefruit and vegetables. Eventually he would have ten acres of
orange and grapefruit groves.

While he was in Florida he entered into a brief but quite
personal correspondence with Sharlot M. Hall, Arizona state
historian. Miss Hall had met Sim in Gallup while on one of
her many field trips to the Indian country. She purchased or
was given a set of his albums of the Nightway at that time.
One of her letters included among other chatty items, a
request, for permission to publish the photographs and manuscript that he had prepared on the dance. Schwemberger

7. *Commercial Hotel, Gallup, New Mexico, ca. 1908.*

gave his permission with the stipulation that his name and copyright would be printed under each photograph.[2]

Through Schwemberger's letters to Hall we learn of his reason for dropping his photography. He found the outdoor life invigorating and gave up photography as a commercial venture because it was too confining. That it was not lucrative may also have been a factor. Although he maintained a darkroom in Florida similar to the one in Gallup, he seldom used it, despite many requests from people to do portraits and commercial works.[3] (He must have had his camera with him too.)

During his communication with Hall, Schwemberger

again displayed his sense of humor. In a jesting way he explained that he was an avowed bachelor because he found it hard to confine his thoughts to just one woman. However, he did indicate that he would like to find someone who would think enough of him to become his wife, and jokingly he concluded that he probably wouldn't have the money for a license.[4]

Sim managed Camp Willard until September 1911, building larger facilities, increasing the farm animal population, and planting citrus groves and vegetable gardens as well as leading hunting parties. Then abruptly, for no apparent reason, he left the rugged nonconfining life in Florida and returned to Arizona, where by September he worked for J. L. Hubbell once again at his newly acquired Cedar Springs Trading Post.[5] He replaced Charles Hubbell, who moved to the Hubbell Trading Post at Oraibi.

The Indian Trader

Cedar Springs in the Hopi Butte country was established as a Hubbell post in 1910, and Charles Hubbell was appointed postmaster there on April 1.

By the end of 1911 the isolation of Cedar Springs began to bother Schwemberger. He had never been isolated from people, and, being the gregarious type, the loneliness was a hardship. He had a limited business ability and was having trouble deciding what to charge for items at the trading post. He was also having difficulty getting his orders filled from the Hubbell supply headquarters in Ganado. He finally expressed his displeasure in December, apparently with no results. There was one bright spot at Cedar Springs, however. On October 20 he was appointed postmaster, a position that gave him added responsibility as well as a small monthly income in addition to his salary from Hubbell.[1]

8. Freighters, ca. 1905.
All supplies for the vast network of trading posts on the Navajo and Hopi reservations were delivered by mule and horse-drawn freight wagons. Here is seen one double wagon and four single wagons en route to one of the Hubbell trading posts.

In addition to the loneliness, Sim was concerned for his life, as he put it, being "done up by the savages." At least his insurance was paid up. But if he should die there he did not want his body sent back to the East. Sim wanted to be "planted any old place in Arizona."[2]

Throughout 1911, Simeon continued to request that J. L. Hubbell visit the post to help him become more proficient in the trading business. In spite of little aggravations, like a leaking roof at the post and his feelings of inadequacy, Simeon remained positive and happy with his new life. This attitude would not last long.

Supplying the far-flung trading post operated by the Hubbells was a difficult and precarious undertaking, as evidenced by the continual concern of Schwemberger over the exclusion of items from his orders. "Navajo with load of goods arrived at 2 P.M. today. I see at a glance that many things ordered were not sent. Where is my coal oil? I'll not do without coal oil in this lonesome place. Where are my saws? Shirts for boys? Bacon? etc., etc., etc., etc., etc., ?[3] By late 1911, correspondence with Ganado, the Hubbell headquarters, was being directed to Roman Hubbell, J. L. Hubbell's youngest son.

The next year, 1912, the year of statehood for Arizona, did not have an auspicious beginning for Simeon and set the stage for some tumultuous times for the estranged Franciscan.

Early that year Schwemberger informed Roman that the Hubbell competitors in the Butte country, Edwin Jacob Marty and Hubert Richardson at Indian Wells, were getting all the wool and corn because "Marty has established a reputation for higher prices so thoroughly that the savages will take the biggest part of their wool from here, to him."[4] Sim was concerned about the lack of faith Roman had in him; when Charles Hubbell had been at Cedar Springs he had a free rein and gave the Navajo considerably more for their corn.[5]

The situation was difficult for Sim to understand: he agreed to do the best he could but considered it all "up hill work" for him. He was understandably discouraged and commented that if he had not promised J. L. Hubbell that he would not quit him he would be many miles from Cedar Springs, where it would have been more pleasant and not so lonesome.[6] He continued to request help with no apparent results.

For some months Sim had been ordering and reordering the same articles and they had not been sent. Sim blamed

Roman for the shortages and for causing the sales accounts to be several hundred dollars below the expected level. Consequently, Roman's neglect had benefitted Indian Wells Trading Post. It also put Sim on the spot as far as trying to explain his lack of goods to the Navajos.[7] Simeon was rightfully concerned since, in his early instruction from J. L. Hubbell, he was told to "keep up your stock and you'll do all right."[8]

The supply situation continued to plague Schwemberger through the winter months of 1912. In March, Cedar Springs received a large shipment of pants along with a large load of onions, none of which were needed. In fact, he had more than he could sell of each commodity. He wrapped the extra pants in a "ten pound" Navajo rug so that it looked like a "fifty pounder" and shipped it back to Ganado.[9] He did not comment on what he did with the onions, but he was philosophical about the order saying that he supposed that Roman had wanted to make up a load for the wagon.

By March Sim's eyes were bothering him to such an extent that he could no longer wait for relief.[10] Finally, in early April, Schwemberger left Cedar Springs to attend to his medical needs. This was the first time in nearly a year that he had been absent from the trading post.

Upon his return, late on April 14, he found a letter from Roman requesting that he come to Ganado at once. He arrived there on April 17.[11] What transpired is pure conjecture since the proceedings were not recorded. Roman may have admonished Sim about his attitude toward the business management at Ganado (meaning Roman), or it could have been about Sim's handling of the business at Cedar Springs.

In early August Simeon challenged the veracity of the postmaster at Ganado. He claimed that pieces of his mail had been lost and others had been detained. He accused the Ganado postmaster of changing the postmark date, a serious charge, reasoning that a letter postmarked "Gallup August 4 should certainly arrive before August 12."[12]

Sim's motivation for his antagonism over the mail delivery may have been prompted by his personal involvement with a young woman in Chicago. He had been writing to someone with whom he wished to keep a low profile, and he had asked Roman to have his personal mail held for him in Gallup.[13] This mysterious correspondent was probably Jeaneatte Murphy, a Catholic girl from Chicago. In late August Simeon ask permission to leave the post for Winslow on the morning of September 10, but gave no details.[14] Hubbell never acknowledged his request.

The only answer received from his query was two letters from Hubbell in which he must have been duly reprimanded for this abusive letter to the Ganado postmaster, who was incidentally Hubbell's nephew. Simeon defended his actions and offered Hubbell the opportunity to view the envelopes in proof of his accusation. He further commented that he had done considerable "kicking" about the mail. Claude, the mail clerk at Ganado, was the only one in charge who acknowledged his letter and also regretfully disclosed having neglected to process the mail properly.[15]

Apparently, Hubbell had expressed concern that Sim would leave his position at the post. Sim responded that he did not understand what Hubbell was referring to since at the time he was hired he had stated that he "would not quit the post." Although he had already received three job offers since beginning to work for Hubbell, he promised to give Hubbell two months notice if he did decide to move.

It is obvious by Sim's response that Hubbell was contemplating a change at the post. This occurred five days before Simeon had planned to leave for Winslow and thence to Gallup to be married on September 16.[16] Hubbell fired Simeon on September 9. Sim expressed surprise at his dismissal but decided to take it "philosophically."[17] He stated his position well and showed no animosity toward the elder Hubbell but remained adamant about his right to criticize the handling of the mail and suggested that Hubbell might hear more about the matter in the future.[18]

Hubbell had given Simeon a month to get his things in order and to move from Cedar Springs. Sim told Hubbell that he would not need the whole month to move and that he should have someone to take over so he could leave there Friday morning, September 27.[19] Sim planned on being married in Gallup on September 16 and then return to Cedar Springs on September 22 with his wife.[20] Five days would be enough time to get his things together and move to Indian Wells where he had obtained employment and lodging.

In addition to his enforced move to Indian Wells, things had not gone well for him in Gallup. When Sim's bride-to-be was informed that they were to be married before a justice of the peace and not in a Catholic ceremony she almost went into hysterics, and only after Simeon, Father Weber, and two physicians calmed her did she go through with the marriage rather than return to Chicago.[21] The wedding took place as planned in the offices of W. R. Cregar, justice of the peace for McKinley County, New Mexico. Simeon was forty-five years old, and Jeaneatte had recently celebrated her twenty-second birthday.[22]

Simeon's return to Cedar Springs with his new bride could not have been pleasant since instead of settling down to married bliss he and his wife had to pack all his belongings and move some seventeen miles to Indian Wells. Once settled, they intended to stay there permanently since Jeaneatte liked Indian Wells better than Cedar Springs.[23]

It was an inauspicious beginning for the newlyweds. Simeon's employment at Indian Wells paid very little and, with another responsibility now, it was more important than ever for him to improve his financial position. Toward the end of the summer he began his attempt to get a traders's license for the reservation. However, this plan was met with intense and bitter opposition. Starting in August 1913 and continuing for the next three months Father Anselm Weber exchanged a series of letters with those who could adversely influence Schwemberger's license application.

Weber considered Schwemberger dishonest and a scamp because of the incidents that took place four years before. Many of Weber's statements in his letters recounted actions by Simeon that occurred prior to and at the time Simeon left the Franciscans in 1909. Among these were Simeon's infatuation with Weber's cousin and his taking the glass-plate negatives and camera. He had also collected some money that was owed the Franciscans for his photographic work. The wounds had not healed. Certainly Weber had grounds for his attitude, but after four years, his action was surprising. Prior to this time Simeon had not been in the vicinity of St. Michaels, but now his proposed location at Fort Defiance was too close for Father Weber. He did everything in his power to dissuade the government officials from granting Schwemberger's request for a trader's license.[24] Many Navajos knew Sim and associated him with the mission, and perhaps Father Anselm thought this would be a detriment to the ongoing missionary work at St. Michaels.

By late August 1913, Simeon was in Gallup and unaware of Weber's attempt to squelch his application. Whether he had left Indian Wells voluntarily or had been released is not known. The president of the C. C. Manning Co. noted in a letter that he had learned that Sim had sent a large load of goods to Fort Defiance and that he would follow the next day to begin work on his store.[25] Apparently, there was no substance to his report.

In the meantime Sim and his wife had been camping out at Fort Defiance for nearly two months, waiting for his trader's license. At this time he did not know that Weber was trying to block his request. Forced into leaving Fort Defiance for Gallup, he soon obtained temporary employment with Joel Higgins McAdams, a Gallup trader and store owner.[26] He was obligated to McAdams only until November 6. So he asked Hubbell for his Cedar Springs job back. Hubbell apparently offered him the job but wanted him sooner that Sim could honestly terminate his employment with McAdams.[27] Sim asked McAdams if he could leave earlier than November 6, but McAdams was adamant and Sim honored his obligation to stay.

Anselm Weber continued to send letters to Charles Lusk, secretary of the Bureau of Catholic Indian Missions and even to Carl Hayden, then Arizona's congressional representative, concerning the license. His continuous letter writing produced results. However, it was two months after the initial application from Schwemberger reached Paquette, superintendent of the Navajo reservation, before the Indian Office reacted. In a telegram to Paquette, Commissioner of Indian Affairs Sells requested a statement from Father Weber listing his charges of dishonesty. In addition, Paquette was to send along Simeon's rebuttal to Weber's charges.

Weber's final words on the subject brought an end to his campaign for he told Lusk that if Sells would not accept his statement without placing it before Schwemberger, then he, Sells, should ignore it. "I am through with this affair and shall not write another letter or bother you again in this disagreeable matter. MUST the Indian Office justify its refusal to HIS [Schwemberger's] satisfaction? That would seem impossible."[28]

Schwemberger's plea for his old job back at Cedar Springs did not go unheeded. By December 1913, and perhaps earlier, he was back at the trading post. Jeaneatte had remained in Ganado for medical reasons.[29] On January 6 she underwent surgery for an undisclosed problem and was not able to return to her husband for some time.

Sim's days at the post were busy and profitable but his nights were lonesome; he declared that he had lost four pounds and was hoping his wife would soon return and take charge of the kitchen.[30] By March, Jeaneatte was back at the post and recuperating nicely.[31]

The year at the post passed uneventfully. Correspondence between the post and Ganado was brisk and mainly business-related with little in the way of personal comment.

At this point in Schwemberger's life he had been a Franciscan brother, a photographer, an Indian trader, and a store proprietor. In early 1915 he added a fifth occupation: the manufacturing of yucca root soap. Yucca roots have been used by Native Americans as a shampoo for centuries. The shampoo's cleaning properties were excellent: the advertisement on the business letterhead proclaimed that yucca root would leave the hair glossy, soft, and lustrous.[32] The enterprise was called the Navajo Ta-La-Wush company with Simeon Schwemberger, Arthur Bailey, and Jeaneatte Schwemberger as partners. The business had been operating for some time prior to this letter as advertisements had been bringing more orders than they could handle. They were unprepared for the popularity of the product.

To date they had invested two hundred dollars of their own money. All the milling was done by hand. Schwemberger noted that he needed an engine to run the mill, but more important they really needed a home. It was Simeon's dream that someday they would have a little store of their own in connection with the Ta-La-Wush business.

The Schwembergers left Cedar Springs in the fall of 1915 and soon after purchased the Gallup store of Eugene Schuster.[33] For the next three years the store took most of the Schwemberger's time.

Around May 7, 1918, Jeaneatte left Gallup for Los Angeles, California. What efforts Sim made to rekindle the lost affection are not known, but he waited a year until he filed for divorce. The grounds were desertion and abandonment.[34] The divorce was granted on May 20, 1919. In a letter to a friend, Mrs. H. H. Hanns, published in the *Gallup Indepen-*

dent, Jeaneatte Schwemberger stated that she would change her name and move to Washington State where she would permanently reside.[35]

In September 1919 Schwemberger moved to his new store which had been under construction for several months. The new location, 221 Wilson Ave., is now the Catholic School, and nothing remains of the once prosperous post. In the 1928 Gallup and McKinley County business directory the store was listed as Sim's Indian Trading Store.[36]

Schwemberger had the post constructed to his specifications and described it as the most convenient store in the Navajo world. On the property to the rear of the store he built a Navajo hogan for the visiting traders. The first day the hogan was completed twenty-five Navajos occupied it during the night. They claimed to have slept without any "unusual dreams" despite the fact that the hogan had not been properly blessed by a Navajo medicine man.[37] Eventually Schwemberger had six hogans to accommodate the increasing number of Indian clients.[38]

The store interior was long and narrow from front to back, with the hay and saddle room attached on the side of the main structure and living quarters at the back. The building was constructed of adobe. Goods were placed on shelves around the wall and a counter extended along one wall and across the end of the building forming an area for people to gather in, shop or just sit; this was called the bullpen.[39]

The store sold goods and also served coffee and food of various types. All the usual items found in trading posts of the day were in ample supply—tobacco, groceries, hay, tack, candy, rugs, tin goods, and pottery.[40] After closing Sim would pull tables out to accommodate any and all who wanted to play cards around the pot-bellied stove. He often entertained with his jew's harp and led lively songs with patrons and friends. It apparently was a warm and hospitable place.

Three years after the new store opened, on January 23, 1923, Simeon, now age fifty-six, married Margaret Sandy of Woodward, Oklahoma, who was twenty years old. They had a daughter, Eunice Adeline. Margaret operated the store until 1941, ten years after Sim's death. There is little record of these years.

The final episode in the life of Simeon Schwemberger begins in March of 1930 with a family auto trip to west-central Florida where Schwemberger visited his brother and his land in Largo, Pinellas County.[41] He still held ten acres of agricultural land, an orange grove, and two lots in the High Point subdivision. The excursion took eight weeks. During this trip Simeon's blood pressure became dangerously high. Upon their return, in late April or early May, he entered the hospital where his health improved, and his blood pressure was stabilized.[42] However, for the next eight months Simeon's health continued to worsen and, in early January, he was once again admitted to St. Mary's hospital. On Saturday, January 17, 1931, he died at the age of sixty-four.[43]

Simeon George Charles Schwemberger spent thirty years in the Southwest, first as a Franciscan brother in the formative years of St. Michaels Mission and the mission efforts of the Catholic church in the New Mexico and Arizona territories. As a photographer he recorded much of the life of the Navajo and added to the visual knowledge of the Rio Grande pueblos. As a postmaster and trader at Cedar Spings he wrote letters that give unusual insight into the operations of an early Hubbell trading post and the difficulties of the frontier trading enterprise. His later years as a proprietor of his own store are not as well documented, but apparently he was quite prosperous.

From his letters and from those who knew him he emerges as a man of principle, a hard worker, and a considerate, friendly, and helpful person. Simeon Schwemberger made a lasting contribution to the history of Arizona and New Mexico with nearly 400 glass-plate negatives taken between 1903 and 1908. Simeon Schwemberger is buried in the Elk's plot at Hillcrest cemetery in Gallup, New Mexico.

The Odyssey

Simeon Schwemberger's estate was left to his second wife, Margaret, and his daughter Eunice, including the glass-plate negatives and a camera, a Burke and James 5 x 7 view camera with a f/7.5 convertible lens.[1]

There is no evidence that Margaret ever printed any of the glass plates. In fact, a conversation with Carmen Charimonte, Margaret's second husband, revealed that the negatives were sold to Peter Havens, a Gallup photographer, "to get them out of the house and their sight."[2] Apparently everything of Simeon's was destroyed except the camera and negatives.

Havens stated that he bought nearly 400 glass-plate negatives and the camera from Charimonte for five dollars.[3] According to Charimonte he disposed of the negatives and camera shortly after his marriage to Margaret.

In either 1937 or 1938 the Franciscan Fathers at St. Michaels took steps to recover the negatives which were rightfully theirs. Havens had informed the Franciscans that he had the glass plates that Schwemberger had taken when he left the mission in 1909. The publicity surrounding the photographs during the interim had been substantial, and consequently the historic value of the glass negatives increased. Legally, the glass plates belonged to the Franciscan Fathers of St. Michaels. Havens sold them back for fifty dollars.[4]

The majority of these plates can be identified as Schwemberger's work, as he inscribed his name, "Simeon Schwemberger" or "Sim," with the date, and the word *copyright* on each negative. Those not so marked were stored in manila envelopes with his name and minor identification on them. Many photographic prints have been located in archival collections which do not have accompanying negatives. The majority are in the Stewart Culin Archival Collection at the Brooklyn Museum.

The recent publication of all of J. B. Moore's catalogs adds more photographs that may have been done by Schwemberger. The illustrations in Moore's 1911 catalog, *The Navajo,* are all Schwemberger's and were taken in 1906, as indicated by the copyright date which partially appears on the photograph reproduced on page 28 of the catalog.[5]

The largest group outside the St. Michaels archives is in the possession of the Museum of Northern Arizona and consists of eighty-one glass negatives from the J. W. Hildebrand collection. Another set belongs to Nello Guadagnoli of Gallup, New Mexico. His collection of forty-eight negatives includes several of the original Nightway series. Guadagnoli made prints from these negatives, and they may be seen in the museum at the Cameron Trading Post.

It is imperative that this collection be preserved. The Franciscans have gone a long way toward saving them, but more needs to be done. All the nitrate film negatives should be duplicated onto safety film, and the glass plates should be treated to arrest the fungus growth and preserved.

The photographs consist of views of the Navajo, Hopi, and Rio Grande people and homes. The better ones are portraits of individuals and family groups. There are also many images of native ceremonies, the best of which are the Nightway sequence.

A small percentage depict activities of the mission and an even smaller number record activities and personnel of the military in the area from time to time. A particularly interesting set documents the military intervention into the Oraibi split of 1906, some which are illustrated in this book (see pages 91–92).

The Night Chant or Nightway[1]

The following series of photographs is a selected collection of the 1905 Night Chant curing ceremony and initiation photographed by Simeon Schwemberger between November 2 and November 15. The completed collection includes forty-eight dry-plate negatives.

The common length of the Night Chant is nine days but on the morning of November 5 the patient's wife commenced her "monthly course." In Navajo culture this is a period of time when no ceremony can be conducted. The morning of November 10 the medicine man returned and resumed the ceremonies, which concluded on the night of November 15.

The medicine man in charge of the ceremony was Hataalii Notgloi (Laughing Singer/Doctor). He appears in several of the photographs. The patient was Hastiin Dilawushy Bitsoi (maternal grandson of the screamer).

According to Schwemberger's manuscript, this particular Night Chant was the first of its kind to be conducted in the vicinity of St. Michaels.

In *Anselm Weber, O.F.M,* Robert L. Wilken details an important historic confrontation that occurred at the conclusion of the 1905 Nightway. A summary of the event follows.

During the last day of the Night Chant, November 15, by arrangement of Father Anselm Weber and Chee Dodge, several headmen spoke to the estimated 2,000 Navajos stressing the need for peace with the government and advised against the use of alcohol at the dance. This "peace talk" was inspired by Weber and Dodge in response to the following situation.

In early November 1905, Reuben Perry, superintendent of the Navajo Agency, had been seized by a group of Navajos after he had opposed the Navajo adjudication of a case of rape. Perry wanted the culprit to stand trial before him in Fort Defiance. The unrest that followed was of great concern to Father Weber. Upon Perry's return to Fort Defiance he met with Father Weber and Chee Dodge. Both Weber and Dodge agreed that Perry had made an error in letting the Navajo get away with violence against the government. Immediately Perry sent for troops from Fort Wingate. Upon their arrival it was agreed that the presence of troops and the volatile feelings of the Navajo would certainly lead to hostilities, so the troops retired to Gallup to await the outcome of the gathering at the Night Chant.

With the large crowd in attendance at the "sing," tensions were high as the headmen circulated among their people. Anselm Weber and Chee Dodge had met with the Navajo leaders prior to the dance to plan their talk with the people. Black Horse and Tayoni also had been invited to attend. Both were critical of Perry's handling of the case and told him that had he depended on the headmen he could have averted the incident.

The various headmen—Black Horse, Tayoni, Qastin Yazhe, Charley Mitchell, and Chee Dodge—spoke to the crowd. The emphasis was on peace with the government and the desire that whiskey would not be consumed at the dance. Apparently the talks were effective since the ceremony was completed without incident.

The text that follows was written shortly after the 1905 St. Michaels Nightway by Simeon Schwemberger and sent to Sharlot M. Hall, Arizona state historian, in early 1911. It is an important document because it gives information about the Nightway heretofore unknown concerning the patient, how the ceremony was sponsored, and the Navajos' reaction to Schwemberger photographing the "sing."[1]

Every year during the months of October, November and December the Navajo Indian Medicine Men are permitted by the rites of their religion to perform the Yebichai (grandfather of the giants) ceremonies over such persons as request it.

These ceremonies are not permitted except for the sick, although the malady need not necessarily be of a serious nature. Another consideration is that the patient has the where-with-all to pay for the ceremonies.

After once they are started the medicine man must complete them, and if for lack of funds or any other reason he must discontinue the ceremonies he is not permitted to start another until the completion of the one he has begun.

These ceremonies cost the patient Two hundred dollars or Two hundred and fifty dollars in all.

Not only does the medicine man demand an exorbitant fee, but every Indian assisting in any way must be provided with food which is no small item when one considers there is a lodge to be built, ground to be cleared, wood and water to be hauled and many other things to be attended to, all of which must be paid for in money, sheep or cattle.

Besides those that work there are always many idlers about who invite themselves to partake of the meals; consequently additional allowance must be made for them.

There had never been a Yebichai Dance in this vicinity, and, although the Navajoes were very anxious to have one, there was no Indian rich enough to bear the expense. An Indian, Hastin Dilawushy Bitsoi (Grandson of the Screamer), was anxious to have the ceremonies over him because his hearing was affected and he believed they would cure him of his malady, but he had already spent much money and many sheep for a "Hatal Unda" (Squaw Dance) over his wife, and was now in financial straits. Mr. Charles L. Day, an Indian trader at St. Michael's, Arizona, informed of this fact and with an eye to business, told one of his friends—a photographer whose specialty is Navajo pictures—that he proposed to help Hastin Dilawushy Bitsoi to have the dance provided he could get a complete set of photographs of the most important ceremonies.

The photographer agreed, for it was quite to his taste although it meant hard work, long hours and a considerable expense, which however he was assured would in time prove a profitable investment. Mr. Day accordingly conferred with the Indian with favorable results, for the Indian, overjoyed at the prospect of having a dance over him, readily consented to the plan.

Mr. Day agreed to have the timbers cut, lodge erected, ground cleared and a stipulated sum of money provided, and the Indian in return promised to allow the photographer to take all the photographs he desired.

This bargain completed, the next move was to engage a medicine man who would not object to the taking of pictures during the ceremonies. As a rule the medicine men are much opposed to photography and even silver fails to induce them to allow the camera to be present during the important ceremonies; so Mr. Day sent for Hatalo Notgloi (Laughing Doctor), a medicine man living near Crystal, New Mexico, who arrived several days later and was Mr. Day's guest during his

9. Erecting the medicine lodge, St. Michaels, October 1905.
Normally the patient's hogan was used for any ceremony, but if the residence was not large enough to accommodate the ceremony a special structure was built for the purpose. In the case of the Night Chant ceremony it was necessary to erect a large hogan.

10. Medicine lodge ready for the covering, St. Michaels, October 1905.
Charles Day hired ten to twelve men to cut the timbers and erect
the medicine lodge. It took them nearly eight days to complete the
task.

stay. Mr. Day explained why he wished to have him hold the
Yebichai dance in this vicinity; that many children were not
initiated and the Indians were very anxious they should be.
He also approached him on the photograph question and met
with no difficulty in obtaining his consent. Part of the money
was to be paid in advance and the balance at the close of the
ceremonies.

The doctor and his patient-to-be arranged the preliminar-
ies. The date decided upon (November 15, 1905) left ample

11. Medicine lodge completed, St. Michaels, November 1905.

time for the erection of the lodge and clearing of the ground. Mr. Day chose the site where the lodge was to be built, and afterwards hired a dozen Indians or thereabouts to cut timbers, etc. It took eight days to complete the work, the Navajos not being noted for their "hustling" ability.

When the lodge was nearly completed the Indians constructed a kitchen out of the brush cut down in clearing the ground, which next day was occupied by the patient's family and many of his female relatives whose duty it is to supply the meals for the medicine man and all other Navajoes that are present during the nine days following. Their task is surely not an enviable one, for they have at times a large crowd to

12. Bearer of the medicine man's paraphernalia, St. Michaels, November 1905.
Traditionally, the medicine man did not carry or prepare his medicine bundle but instead had several apprentices to arrange and
transport the paraphernalia.

13. Laughing Singer, St. Michaels, November 1905.
Hataalii Notgloi (Laughing Doctor) was the singer in charge of the
St. Michaels Night Chant. The "singer" is the man of medicine.
His skill, knowledge, and past success with certain rites determine
his demand as a singer. When it is known that his medicine pouch
contains items of antiquity that are difficult to obtain or that he has
been successful in curing certain diseases, the demand for his services increases.

14. The kitchen occupied, St. Michaels, November 1905.
With the large attendance of relatives, friends, and others at the major curing ceremonies it was the responsibility of the patient's family to feed all the guests. Consequently, large kitchen areas were established to prepare food for the attendees. Large five-gallon cans and buckets were used to cook the food. Sandstone slabs placed over hot fires were used to cook meat and corn cakes.

15. The bread maker, St. Michaels, November 1905.

feed, especially during the last three days when fifteen or twenty gallons of coffee are often required at one meal.

During these ceremonies the Indians always feast, and should perchance the supply of provisions fall short it would be a standing rebuke to the patient forever after.

The day previous to the completion of the lodge a Navajo was sent to the doctor to notify him that all would be in readiness for him to open the ceremonies the next night. The following day he arrived, accompanied by the Indian carrying his paraphernalia at the rear of his saddle. The medicine man never carries his own paraphernalia. If it is not sent for before he is notified by the Navajo that all is in readiness, the Navajo must pack the load himself.

This particular carrier arrived at the lodge at sunset and deposited the masks, feathers, rattles and medicines upon the skins that were placed on the ground floor to receive them.

After dark the doctor arrived at the lodge (for the medicine man never enters the lodge until the masks have been placed therein), and was greeted pleasantly by all the Indians. After a short chat with them he sat on the skins which the patient had provided for him and began to smoke the tobacco which was also furnished by the patient.

During these ceremonies the medicine man is monarch; his word is law. Yet it requires some diplomacy on his part to insure a successful termination of the ceremonies.

Those who assist him do so voluntarily, although at times the assistance of many others is required.

The first of the series of ceremonies which are to continue for nine days is begun by preparing rings of cedar boughs. The patient is not permitted to enter the lodge until one of these has been placed upon his head. Two Indians mask themselves to impersonate certain gods. They leave the lodge followed by all the Indians except the doctor. In a few moments the doctor commands everyone to enter the lodge, the patient following at the end of the procession. After the patient has been seated the god impersonators enter and remove the ring from his head, when another is placed upon his head amidst the chanting of the doctor and various ceremonies. This is repeated ten times, and no one is permitted to leave or enter the lodge during this ceremony. After the ceremony (at about 11:30 p.m.) those present enjoy a sumptuous meal of coffee, tortillas, mutton, potatoes, onions and pumpkin.

The medicine man and the patient must remain in the lodge all night. Others may remain if they wish, but no one is allowed to sleep between the medicine man and the patient, and the women are forbidden to enter.

On the morning of the second day the patient may go wherever he may wish, but he must be present during the ceremonies. After the morning repast preparations are begun for the sweat house ceremony. Stones of various colors are gathered, a metate secured, and all placed in the lodge. The stones are reduced to powder on the metate, and each color placed on a piece of bark.

About three hundred feet east of the lodge a sweat house is constructed. In front of it a fire is kindled over some stones which are to be placed inside when thoroughly heated. At noon the doctor comes and orders a smooth place to be made about three inches wide, extending from the bottom of the north side to the bottom of the south side and from the top down on the west side. Two Indians then make the "Satsini Ekah" (Rainbow in sand) on the smooth surface, the doctor superintending the work.

The patient is sent for, and whilst he undresses the stones are placed in the sweat house. The doctor then sprinkles sacred meal on them and the patient crawls in, clad only in the "G" string. Blankets are then placed over the entrance, and the doctor, after sticking bunches of feathers around the sweat house, sits on the ground nearby and begins his chant which lasts about forty-five minutes.

Two impersonators of gods now advance, hooting "Hoo-oo-oo-oo-ooh!" They lift the blankets, when the patient crawls forth and sits on a blanket near by. The god impersonators continue their hooting and fantastic gestures for ten minutes, after which they return to the timber.

The doctor hands the patient a lotion which he proceeds to use. After he has dressed himself, the doctor strews some sacred meal on the ground upon which the patient walks, the doctor and all spectators following, single file, into the lodge.

The doctor starts to chant again, and rattles a gourd containing bits of turquoise and shells. Near the end of the chant

16. Metate and colored stones, St. Michaels, November 1905.
The medicine man's paraphernalia included colored stones from
which the sands are derived for drypainting, the grinding stones for
producing the sands, and pieces of bark that held the sands while
the painting is being made. In the middle and left background are
long juniper paddles, which are actually weaving batons borrowed
from the weaver to smooth the sand on which the drypainting is
produced.

17. Near view of the sweat-house, St. Michaels, November 1905.
The sweat-house is a miniature conical hogan with the doorway
structure omitted. The "sudatory" is used in various ceremonies.
In the Night Chant four sweat-houses are erected at each of the
cardinal points. On four consecutive days the patient enters one of
the sweat-houses starting on the east and finishing on the north by
way of the south and west. During this process the singer decorates
the lodge with a figure representing the rainbow. When the draw-
ing of the rainbow in completed the patient enters the sweat-house.

he puts pollen on the feet, hands, shoulders, neck and head of the patient. He then places some upon his own head and a pinch upon his tongue. He likewise gives the patient a pinch of pollen on his tongue and then passes the pollen bag to those present, each Indian putting a small quantity upon his head and his tongue, one passing the bag to the other untill all have partaken, after which all the Indians present help themselves to the food brought in.

There are no more ceremonies until after sunset. Usually the ceremonies at night do not start before nine or ten o'clock.

On the second night the patient is covered with spruce boughs; that is, the spruce is attached to his clothing from head to foot. While the god impersonators are removing it with arrow heads and stone knives the doctor and several Indians are chanting and beating an inverted ceremonial basket. After the spruce has been removed the god impersonators cut it into small pieces over the patient's head.

On the third day before sunrise one Indian is sent from the lodge with an eagle feather which he fastens to a pinyon sapling. It remains there all day, but no one touches it. The sweat house ceremony takes place early in the morning, the same sweat house being used but instead of a sand painting it is decorated with pine boughs. The ceremonies are the same as those of the preceding day.

In the lodge a "Tadidin Ashki Ekah" (Pollen Boy in sand) is made. Quite a ceremony is held over the patient at the edge of the painting, and he is then requested to sit upon it. The doctor chants and rattles his gourd: after some time elapses a god impersonator enters and sits near the patient. When the doctor has finished his chant the god impersonator hoots over the patient and continues a series of gestures lasting about ten minutes.

This is one of their most sacred ceremonies, and no one is permitted to enter or leave the lodge while it lasts. Many were surprised to see a photographer there with his camera, and

18. Pollen Boy sandpainting, St. Michaels, November 1905.
On the second day of the Night Chant this drypainting is created.
The four sacred mountains of the Navajo are represented by conical
piles of colored sand. Faint lines lead from the mountains to the
central figure, indicating trails of the succoring gods. From the
southeast to the center is a line of corn meal. Along its course are
four footsteps. It marks the trail of Haashch'ee l ti'i and the patient.
The person sung over must walk exactly in the footsteps of the god
if he is to recover.

19. Patient sitting on sandpainting, St. Michaels, November 1905.
The patient sits on the sandpainting described in Figure 15.

more so when he placed it upon the tripod. Objections were raised by the Indians, but the doctor and his patient seemed not to hear them. Just what the result would have been had they directly accosted the doctor for permitting this offense, is hard to say.

The photographer made several exposures, but the light was poor, and the smoke pouring out of the only opening did not serve to help matters. However he obtained satisfactory results, and prizes the pictures very highly as they are the first and only ones in existence, and may perhaps never be secured again.

20. Coming out of the sweat-house, St. Michaels, November 1905.

21. Coming out of the sweat-house, near view, St. Michaels, November 1905.

22. After the sweat, St. Michaels, November 1905.
The patient is seated on a blanket where the medicine man and the male Ye'ii administer to him after the sweat bath. This ritual takes place on each of the first four days of the Night Chant.

After sunset the tree to which the feather is attached is cut down and laid over the entrance to the lodge, and the doctor commands all persons to enter. The patient comes in last and sits on a sheep skin facing the east. A hole is dug in front of him into which the doctor sprinkles sacred meal. The god impersonators enter bringing the tree with them, and plant it in the hole prepared for it. A mask is placed over the patient's head, and many long and weird ceremonies take place. At last the tree is bent over the patient and the mask fastened to it

23. After the bath in yucca suds, St. Michaels, November 1905.
"This ceremony is similar to the one depicted in Figure 19. The
patient however removes all his clothes except the loincloth, and
while the medicine men are chanting he washes himself in suds
prepared by an Indian with the crushed roots of the yucca plant. He
then washes his beads and then he rubs his body with meal and then
sits on the blanket until the ceremony is finished."

with a buckskin string. The god impersonators then raise the tree and carry it out, after which they remove the mask and feather and place the tree above the entrance again, the mask and feather being returned to the lodge.

Those who are to take part in the dance on the ninth night leave the lodge after they have partaken of their repast, and practice the Yebichai dance. This they must rehearse every night, though masks are not permitted during the rehearsals.

On the fourth day the sweat house ceremony and sand painting are the same as on the second day. After this ceremony another weird and most interesting one takes place in the lodge. While the patient sits on some skins an Indian in front of him makes suds in a ceremonial basket with crushed Yucca root and water. Making suds in a basket may seem strange to an Easterner, but the Navajos not only make baskets and jugs to hold water but some of their blankets are water-tight as well. After the suds are quite stiff the doctor takes some pollen and makes a broad line on the suds from east to west and another from north to south, then another all along the edge of the basket. Many other ceremonies are performed over the suds, at the end of which the patient removes all his clothing except the "G" string. While the doctor is chanting the patient washes his own body with the suds, then his beads; and after he has poured the last drop on his head he rubs himself with sacred meal and sits on a blanket until the chanting has ceased. He then dons his clothing without removing the meal that adheres to him.

No protests were made when the photographer took views of this ceremony. Evidently the Indians had seen the uselessness of the protests on the previous day.

At night a row of masks are exposed and many ceremonies performed over them. The masks are repeatedly sprinkled with water and smoke puffed on them. All inmates of the lodge participate in the ceremony, sticking their fingers in the water and sucking them, making a loud noise in so doing.

24. The first large sandpainting, St. Michaels, November 1905.
"Many years have elapsed since this sandpainting was produced and many years may pass before it is used again. This painting occupies all the floor available, only a narrow passage on the sides is left. Almost a day was required to finish it although eight or ten Indians were constantly at work." *Quoted from Schwemberger's album.*

   This sandpainting is made on the seventh day and is often called the Talking god/Calling (Harvest or Hogan) god drypainting.

61

The walls are also repeatedly sprinkled with water. A long ceremony is then performed over the patient by masked men. As usual a sumptuous meal is spread and the dance rehearsed.

On the fifth day the last sweat house ceremony takes place. It is identical with that of the third day. In the lodge the patient repeats long prayers recited by the doctor which last about half an hour and become extremely monotonous. At the end of the prayers the doctor rubs pollen on the patient's feet, hands, shoulders and head and gives him a pinch of pollen on his tongue.

On the sixth day all is bustle early in the morning, for a large sand-painting must be started and finished before sunset. Several blanket-loads of common sand are emptied on the floor from west to east. This is smoothed down nicely and the artists begin the center figure. More sand is brought in as required, and an Indian is kept busy reducing the stone to powder on the metate to keep the bark dishes replenished. At times twelve or fifteen men are at work on one painting. The doctor remains in the lodge until the painting is completed unless there happens to be another medicine man present who understands directing so large a piece of work, in which case he usually asks him to superintend it; and, this being considered an honor, the second medicine man complies gladly.

Not all Navajos are adept at sand-painting. Some few are experts at the work, and such are always chosen to do the principal outlining. A pinch of sand (pulverized stone) dexterously applied will make a distinct and even line an eighth of an inch wide and about three inches long. It is beyond my ability to explain intelligently the wonders and beauty of a well-executed sand-painting. These immense drawings, symbolic of Indian deities, with all their crudity preserving a certain symmetry of line, striking in color contrasts of black, red, blue, white, gray, half Egyptian in character yet wholly barbaric and peculiar alone to the American Indian, form a fine mosaic which it is a lasting pity to obliterate. I had hoped

25. The Food Solicitors, St. Michaels, November 1905.
"The most difficult of all the photos to get was this one. Three
Indians, masked to represent certain gods, leave the lodge early in
the morning and go from dwelling to dwelling in quest of food for
those taking part in the ceremonies; they must do this even if it is
very cold or the ground covered with snow; they are not allowed to
remain quiet for a second, and if they notice anyone approaching
them with a camera they turn "back to" and spread out so it is
impossible to get even a fairly good snapshot. They are not permitted to speak while masked or they will go blind; that is their belief."

the photographer would obtain good results from his negatives of the sand-paintings, but owing to their great breadth not even a wide-angled lens would have embraced them.

During the execution of this painting another ceremony is taking place. Early in the morning three god impersonators had left the lodge, two of them clothed only in a coat of paint, breech-cloth, moccasins and mask; the other in addition to his ordinary dress donning a buckskin apron. Their toilet completed, they go to the nearest Dine bagan (Navajo hut). When within hearing distance the one wearing the apron hoots several times,—the only sound allowed under the mask, a sound which notifies the inhabitants of their arrival so that the children may have time to hide, as they are not permitted to gaze upon the gods. They are taught that these impersonators are actual gods and if they look at them something terrible will happen.

The god impersonators carry small skin bags with them into which the inhabitants must put food, tobacco, or money. Leaving this hut they proceed to the next one, which may be only a few hundred yards distant or several miles. The Indians are great travellers, and walking or running eighteen or twenty miles is not at all unusual with them. The god impersonators are not allowed to remain quiet for a moment, and if they speak while masked they will go blind at once.

As often as their food sacks are filled they are emptied into a blanket and the occupant of the hut must have it carried to the kitchen of the lodge. No matter how inclement the weather may be this ceremony must take place and those who are asked to impersonate these gods dare not refuse. I have known these beggars to travel many miles through a deep December snow, and they are neither permitted to enter a hut or to tarry at a fire.

After they have completed the circuit outlined by the medicine man they return to the lodge, and from thence to a brush enclosure where the children are waiting to be initiated. It is

26. The first initiation, St. Michaels, November 1905.
The figure with the yucca whip, Talking god, is applying strokes to
a male initiate. The female Ye'ii carries a bag of corn pollen, which
is applied to the initiate in certain places as prescribed by the ritual.
After each application the Talking god whips the initiate at those
locations. During the whipping the youths are told not to look up
and must wait their turn with bowed heads. Girls are not whipped;
instead the Talking god presses an ear of white and yellow corn
decorated with spruce against the same places that the boys are
whipped.

27. Talking god at initiation of youth, St. Michaels, November 1905.
The initiation of the youth is a particularly important aspect of the
Night Chant. This can occur on either the sixth, seventh, or eighth
day of the sing, traditionally in the afternoon.

Both boys and girls are initiated at this time. Notice boys and
girls seated in the rear with their heads bowed. They are not
allowed to look at the masked gods.

the day of all days to the Navajo children, for after the initiation they may see all the ceremonies and gaze upon the gods!

The boys remove all their clothing except the "G" string, and sit in line around the enclosure. The girls enter the enclosure arrayed in new dresses, blankets and other fineries, and sit next to the boys. They gaze upon the ground and never once look up, for it would be a sad mistake if they should accidentally see one of the gods. The initiators have been waiting in the near-by shrubbery, and when informed that the children are ready they signal their approach by several hoots. The first initiator lays his hands on the first boy in line. Some of the spectators tell the boy to arise, when sacred meal is placed on his arms, chest, back and legs by one of the initiators, the other crossing these parts with yucca leaves, after which the spectators tell the boy to sit down. Each boy in turn receives the same treatment.

The form used for the initiation of the girls is quite different. Two ears of corn are placed at the feet, hands, breast and head, and then pollen applied to these parts. After all the girls have been treated the children are told they may look at the gods, which they gladly do though some are frightened at the hideous masks. The gods now remove their masks and the children behold the impersonators. They are then instructed in the making of the masks and other mythological rites. This ceremony is completed by putting a mask over each child's head, but care must be taken to adjust it properly for if a child fails to see through the openings left for the eyes he will go blind. The mask is then placed on the ground and each child must sprinkle sacred meal on it. Here again care must be taken, for if a grain of this meal falls through one of the eyes of the mask the child will go blind in that eye.

About three hundred Navajo men and women witnessed this ceremony. The women were very loud in their denunciations of the photographer and the situation looked unpleasant

28. Second large sandpainting, St. Michaels, November 1905.
The original drypainting is about ten feet wide and thirteen feet
long. Only about half of the drypainting is seen in this view. The
figures next to the corn stalk are Fringemouths. The marks on their
bodies and limbs are those of white zigzag lightening. Each of the
Fringemouths carries in his right hand a gourd rattle ornamented
with two circles of plumes and in his left hand a bow ornamented
with plumes and breath feathers. The bow is painted in two colors
to correspond with the body of the bearer. The outer figures seen at
the top left is the Humpback deity. The figures next to the Fringe
mouths are Ye'ii Ba'aad or goddesses.

29. Fringe mouth administers to the patient on the last day of the Night Chant, St. Michaels, November 1905.

for a while, but fortunately he did not open his tripod until the initiators had announced themselves, for as soon as they arrive the women are not permitted to speak and the men knew from former experience that it was useless to protest. The doctor looked through the camera after it had been focused and expressed himself well pleased with what he saw.

Immediately after the initiation another ceremony takes place in the lodge. The patient stands on the sandpainting, which had been finished during the initiation. The doctor gives him a medicated water to drink, after which the god impersonators dance around him, hooting constantly, one after another approaching him and yelling into his ears. This

30. Participants gather for the ninth day of the ceremony, St. Michaels, November 1905.

The ninth day of the ceremony is a gala one for the Navajos who come to the lodge from miles around to gossip, greet old friends, and participate in sports events. Horse racing and foot racing are among the most popular events; along with a "chicken pull" and wild burro race, they keep the attendees busy for most of the day. The final episode of the Night Chant is the public dance by fourteen masked dancers.

At this particular ceremony Schwemberger estimates that 2,500 people came from as far as 100 miles to participate.

ceremony, which lasts about twenty minutes, is a weird and unusual scene.

The ceremonies of the seventh and eighth days are, figuratively speaking, the same as those of the sixth. The three food solicitors sally forth, but go in different directions. The initiations take place after each trip. The sand-paintings are of the same size, but each day are of a different design and, consequently, significantly different also. It would require several large volumes to depict minutely these mythological ceremonies. Every gourd, feather, stone, as well as all maneuvers, gestures and songs, have a significant meaning.

The ninth day is a gala day for the Navajos who come to the lodge in bands from all directions,—some of them from a distance of seventy-five or one hundred miles. Mr. Day's popularity among the Indians caused an unusually large gathering of Navajos on this occasion. The doctor's assistants commenced early in the morning to prepare the masks and other things for the great dance which takes place at night. The only ceremony over the patient takes place at sunset in front of the lodge. It is very short, but once seen it will never be forgotten for it is one of the most fantastic ceremonies ever witnessed.

During the day the patient is kept busy shaking hands and greeting old friends, some of whom he has perhaps not seen for years. His particular friends he invites to the kitchen, where the feasting continues nearly all day. The Navajos do not expect to be fed at the patient's expense on this day; only the specially invited ones and those assisting the doctor must be supplied with food, which however is sufficient to keep the kitchen mechanics busy.

Early in the afternoon the sports begin. A long, level tract of land is selected, about a mile north of the lodge, for the races. Here men, women and children congregate; some to participate in the races, some to bet on them, and others only to see them. Several races were on the program between the best horses. Unlike the eastern races, however, more than two horses, two men or two boys never run in a race. When two horses are to race some one in the crowd announces it: Mr. Short Have's bay mare will race with Mr. Black Rock's four-year-old. The betting starts at once. Everything of any value is a betting article. Blankets, rings, beads, etc., and not seldom horses and saddles, are bet, leaving the loser a chance to count the steps to his hut which may be over the mountain. Yet he is sure to take it philosophically: it is not their custom to brood over their loss, neither do they make a display in times of great luck.

The women also bet on the races and are at times very noisy about it.

The weight of the jockey is never considered: he may be a man or a boy. Saddles are not used, and the only clothing worn by the rider is the "G" string.

They ride slowly to the starting point, from which they start without a signal. The horse passing over the line first wins the race, and the bets exchange hands. There is never any squabbling about the start.

The foot races are also interesting. Stripped of all clothing except the "G" string, the contestants walk slowly to the starting point. Sometimes an Indian accompanies them in order to give the starting signal, but this they seldom do; usually they do their own starting.

The chicken-pulling is the most exciting as well as the most dangerous sport indulged in by the Navajos. A hole is dug in the race-track, and a chicken buried in it up to its neck. The Indians are to ride by at full speed, reach down and pull it out. It is a free-for-all sport, and saddles may be used. Those wishing to participate in the game bunch together on their horses at a distance of about one hundred yards. Single file and at a gallop they ride toward the chicken. Each one in passing reaches down in the endeavor to pull the chicken out. If no one succeeds in the attempt they race for it again, and repeat the performance until one of them succeeds in pulling the chicken out by the neck.

The Navajos are great horsemen. Many would have received fatal injuries at this sport were it not for their agility. The entire weight on one stirrup may cause it to break, or—what happens more frequently—the saddle turns, precipitating the rider. The danger in this sport can be more easily imagined than described, when we realize that there are fifteen or twenty Indians trying their skill and hoping to be the winner of the chicken and the five dollars which some store-keeper has offered as a prize to the lucky man.

The last event is always a free-for-all burro race. The announcement of such a race is hailed with joyous shouts, for it means fun for old and young. These small animals are naturally slow, often stubborn, and always timid. This race is also prompted by a store-keeper, a dollar being the reward to the one passing over the line first. In a crowd of several hundred Indians there are sure to be three or four mounted on burros. These are brought forth, and if the rider happens to be a woman she dismounts, permitting some man or boy to ride the burro. All burros are eligible. If they are minus an ear or two or are without a tail, showing that they have received punishment at the hands of their owners for grazing in forbidden pastures such as corn fields or melon patches, it makes no difference.

Saddles are permitted in this race, and the riders do not disrobe. After kicking the burros in the ribs and using their quirts on the burros' haunches, the race starts slowly. All may go well for twenty-five or fifty feet. By that time, however, at least one of the burros will surely decide for himself that a slow walk is fast enough. This sets the Indians to yelling and laughing, which has the effect of stopping the other burros that were going along nicely. The riders, anxious to win the dollar, use every conceivable means to urge their steeds onward, sometimes dismounting and returning with a big stick (a la Roosevelt) which they proceed to use dexterously if not gracefully. No one has ever timed a burro race with a chronograph. A steeple clock would answer the purpose admirably, but the nearest one is several hundred miles away.

As soon as one of the burros passes over the line the Indians whoop and yell. They then walk or ride to their destinations, most of them returning to the lodge where timber is plentiful and where small fires are built and the evening meal prepared. The kitchen connected with the lodge is abandoned after the doctor and his assistants have partaken of a good meal about the middle of the afternoon, which meal must suffice until the next morning unless they dine with some of their friends during the evening.

The scene about the lodge during the night is very picturesque. Dozens of fires burn amidst the stately pines, around which groups of Navajos sit smoking and talking, while the horses neigh, the asses bray and the dogs bark. It is an impressive picture. On this occasion it was especially so as there were about two thousand five hundred Indians present. The first ceremony began at half past eight.

Five masked men arrived at the lodge entrance, four of them being the dancers, and the fifth the "Ye" or giant who does the hooting. The doctor and the patient emerge from the lodge, when the doctor sprinkles sacred meal on each of them, after which he recites prayers which are repeated by the patient. After the prayers had been said and sacred meal sprinkled on the dancers, the "Ye" hooted and the dancers sang and danced, half of the time dancing toward the east and the other half toward the west. After the dance they returned to the enclosure, where they removed their masks and dressed themselves.

About half-past nine large fires were kindled at the dance place. Several American men and women from Gallup, New Mexico, and Fort Defiance, Arizona, had arrived. The Indians do not solicit the presence of white people, but when they are present the chiefs always provide a good site for them and have logs brought that they may sit comfortably.

Those that are to participate in the coming dances meet in an enclosure near the sweat house where they disrobe and paint their bodies. After the paint has dried they don richly ornamented breech cloths, silver belts, beads, bracelets, rings, and fox skins attached to the back of the breech cloths. They then put the mask over their heads and march single file to the dance place, headed by the "Ye" who does the hooting to notify all to make room for them.

The doctor and the patient come out of the lodge again, the preliminary ceremony being practically the same as with the four dancers. The patient goes down the line of the fourteen dancers, sprinkling meal on each one, and, returning on the other side, does the same. The "Ye" hoots twice, and the dancers commence to sing and dance most fantastically. When the song is nearly completed they turn eastward and finish the song on their way out of the enclosure.

In a few minutes they return and repeat the same song and dance. This repetition continues all night, the only change being in the dancers, of whom there are several relays.

During the dance there is also a ceremony taking place in the lodge, where twelve or fifteen medicine men and singers keep up a continuous chant all night, and there the patient spends the greater part of his time. The last song, "Dali Ani" (Blue Bird), takes place just before sunrise. This song is somewhat different from those sung during the night, though the dance is the same.

After this dance has been finished there are no more ceremonies and the singing in the lodge also ceases.

THE PHOTOGRAPHS

31. Brother Arnold, Brother Simeon Schwemberger, and Mr. Duran.
This photograph may have been taken by Elizabeth Funk with
Simeon's help.

32. Exercising the franchise, ca. 1907.

This could be any of a number of elections between 1903 and 1908. Sammy Day is seated with his back to the camera and with a Colt revolver on hip. Frank Walker, Simeon Schwemberger, Father Anselm Weber, and Dan Mitchell complete the group.

33. Our camp at Oraibi.
Left to right: Simeon Schwemberger, Elizabeth Funk, unidentified woman, and W. E. Hildebrand.

34. Lunch time.
Simeon Schwemberger and John Osbourne pause for lunch along
the trail in Navajo country.

35. Reuben Perry and J. Flanders, Fort Defiance, 1906.
Perry was superintendent of the Navajo reservation during the trying times with the Hopi and Flanders assistant superintendent. Perry figured prominently in the settlement of Navajo disturbances in 1905 and later became the government agent at Zuni.

36. Winter quarters, St. Michaels, October 1906.
Captain S. N. Holbrook and Lieutenant J. H. Lewis were the
officers sent from Fort Wingate to Oraibi to support Reuben Perry
in his attempt to re-establish order among the Hostiles and Friendlies. The two troops of cavalry spent two nights at St. Michaels
during a snowstorm before continuing to Oraibi.

37. Theodore G. Lemmon, Superintendent of the Hopi,
Keams Canyon, ca. 1906.

Lemmon became superintendent of the Hopi in 1904 and was in charge during the Oraibi Split of September 8, 1906. Much of the literature on the Hopi blames the division of Oraibi, known as the Split, on the differences created by the acceptance or non-acceptance of Anglo-American ways. Actually the dissension had existed for generations as the Bear and Spider clans struggled for control of the political and religious activities of the village. Coupled with this difficulty was the changing environment along Oraibi wash, which may have further caused internal strife, eventually leading to dissension, by changing the distribution of farmable land. The intrusion of the U.S. government with programs for education, land allotments, missionary efforts, and other controls totally foreign to the Hopi was the final blow that divided Oraibi. Each Hopi had to decide which faction he would follow. Husbands and wives, children and parents were torn asunder, clans fractured, and the village split forever.

38. Oraibi, 1906.

39. Walpi from the south.

40. Hopi madonna, 1906.

The cradleboard is made by Third Mesa craftsmen. Note the walking stick or staff on the left. These staffs were used not only for support while walking but also for balance while carrying water from the springs at the foot of the mesa to the top of the escarpment where the village was located. The trail was steep, and the water jars held perhaps five gallons of water weighing about forty pounds.

41. Old Hopi woman, standing, Oraibi, Third Mesa, 1906.

42. "The new village of the hostile Hopi, ca. 1907.
The establishment of Hotevilla as the village of the hostiles was motivated by the split at Oraibi over the U.S. government's demand that the Hopi children attend government schools. To the Hopi any government intervention, be it compulsory education, sanitation, or economic controls, was a threat to their independence and the traditional way of life they had enjoyed for centuries.

*43. Agent Perry explains the demands of the government to the
Friendly Men at Oraibi.*

Reuben Perry, superintendent of Fort Defiance Agency, at the time,
was appointed supervisor for the Hopi in October 1906. He was
sent to Oraibi to re-establish order between the Hostiles and the
Friendlies. Soon after Perry's appointment two troops of cavalry
under Captain E. H. Holbrook left Fort Wingate to lend support to
Perry's mission. They stopped two nights at St. Michaels to wait
out a snowstorm.

44. The deposed Hopi chief with the soldiers at Oraibi, 1906.

45. The Friendly chief at Oraibi, ca. 1907.
Wilson Tawaquaptewa, chief of the Friendlies, was just assuming
the chieftainship for Loloma at the time this photograph was taken.

46. Lorenzo's store at Keams, Keams Canyon, Arizona, ca. 1906.

47. Trading Post at Round Rock.
This was Father Leopold's first mission at Round Rock and now is
Garcia's Trading Post.

48. Dine Tsosi, Slim Navajo, last of the Navajo war chiefs, 1906. Dine Tsosi, the last of the Navajo war chiefs, was the grandson, Narbona. Tsosi led the Navajos in many fights against the Comanches, Apaches, Utes, Pueblos, and Mexicans. When he was banished to Fort Sill he and his brother broke away from the soldiers during the night. Once back he continued to lead expeditions against other Indians. On one occasion Colonel Dodd threatened to put him in jail, but Dine Tsosi showed him his numerous wounds, telling Dodd that jail held no threat for one who had faced death so often.

49. Hashke Yazhe, 1907.

50. Charlie Mitchell, Navajo headman.

Father Juvenal Schnorbus enlisted the support of Charlie Mitchell (Tso) early in 1900 to gain support for the St. Michaels school. Mitchell visited the mission in February 1900 and was curious about the Franciscans. He brought Peshlakai (Old Silversmith) and Chee Dodge, both influential headmen, to meet the fathers. Mitchell had been in the contingent that visited the Chicago World's Fair in 1893 with Lieutenant Edwin H. Plummer. He had returned with a liberal outlook on education. Along with Peshlakai and Dodge, Mitchell was instrumental in gaining support for the children of the Navajo to attend boarding school in Santa Fe.

99

51. Chee Dodge, famous Navajo headman, St. Michaels, ca. 1905.

52. Old Silversmith, St. Michaels, ca. 1905.

53. Navajo scouts, St. Michaels, November 16, 1906.

54. The sheep dipping brigade, St. Michaels, 1906.
Navajos and Anglos cooperate in the necessary activity of sheep
dipping. Sheep were dipped to kill pests that infested the wool and
caused scabies; also it helped to keep the wool clean.

55. Stone masons at St. Michaels.

56. *The Day boys and several St. Michaels Mission school students, 1907.*
Sammy, Charley, and Willie Day in the back with the first Navajo
pupils at St. Michaels. Charlie Yazzi and Albert Slinky flank "Blind
Luke." St. Michaels boarding school was in operation by December 3, 1902, the feast of St. Francis Xavier. The Sisters of the
Blessed Sacrament arrived on October 19, 1902. In its first year of
operation the school enrolled twenty-one Navajo students aged
eight to twelve years.

57. *Navajo family, Fort Defiance.*

58. Louis Watchman, wife, and child, St. Michaels, ca. 1905.

59. Navajo man and child, St. Michaels, ca. 1905.

60. Navajo woman and child, St. Michaels, ca. 1905.

61. Navajo medicine man.

62. Navajo girl, September 12, 1902.

63. Carding wool for a Navajo rug.

64. Navajo outfit.

At this summer camp of a Navajo family, a large loom has been erected on which a Navajo rug will be woven. Three to five women will work together on the loom. Dutch ovens cool by the fire.

65. The gathering.

Navajo families travel for miles to attend the important curing ceremonies that are a part of their culture. The large ceremonial hogan is at the left while the visitors wagons delineate the perimeter of the dance area.

66. Wagons gathered at Laguna pueblo for a summer ceremony.

67. Laguna pueblo dancers on the plaza.

68. Jemez pueblo plaza during dance.

69. Pueblo house at Jemez.
Chili and multiple rows of corn on the roof dry in the southwestern sun.

70. Feast day of San Diego, Jemez pueblo.

71. Jemez pueblo.

72. Jemez, coming down the ladder.

73. Jemez pueblo, drummers and dancers on the plaza.

74. Jemez, dancers in the street.

75. Jemez family, ca. 1906.

76. Jemez water girls.
These girls carry pots from (left to right) Acoma, Acoma or Laguna, and Zia. Pots were a common trade item between pueblos.

77. Jemez girl filling her water jar.

78. Jemez pueblo girl.

79. Rio Grande pueblo girl, Lenore Yepa,
one of the first mission school pupils, ca. 1906.

The clothing and jewelry worn by this young woman were re-
served for ceremonies and other festive occasions. Jewelry is important to the Pueblo Indians not only as an economic indicator but
also as a social statement.

A variety of materials is represented in the necklaces worn by
this girl. Shell, turquoise, coral, and silver beads hang around her
neck. Two of the most obvious necklaces are of silver beads. Both
have double-barred cross pendants at the bottom of the strands.
One of the necklaces is called a cross necklace because it has small
single-barred crosses interspersed between the silver beads. The
other has squash blossom beads placed between the round silver
beads. One of the cross pendants has the sacred heart.

The double-barred cross, the cross of Saint James, patron saint of
Spain, is perhaps the most popular form with the Zuni and Rio
Grande people. John Adair suggests that this popularity derives
from the similarity it has to the traditional Pueblo representation of
Dragon Fly.

In addition to the silver necklaces, she is wearing several chokers
of coral, two white shell necklaces, one a fetish type, the other the
simple round shell variety interspersed with large nuggets of turquoise. She also wears a four-strand turquoise and a single-strand
coral necklace. Two hammered silver bracelets adorn her wrist.

80. Acoma pueblo.

81. Acoma pueblo, the Catholic mission church.

82. The Catholic mission church at Cochiti, 1906.

83. Interior of the Catholic mission church at Cochiti pueblo, 1906.

84. Stable, Cochiti pueblo.

85. Bread oven and baker.

86. The governor of Cochiti and his family, 1906.

87. Santiago Quintana, governor of Cochiti, 1906.

88. Crispina, Keres woman, and child, 1906.

89. Margarita and child, Cochiti, New Mexico, 1906.
This mother and child also appear in Figure 86 and may be the wife
of the governor, Santiago Quintana.

90. Victoria with child, Cochiti, New Mexico, 1906.

91. Cochiti Indian women dancers, 1906.

92. Cochiti grandmother and grandchildren, Cochiti, New Mexico, 1906.

93. Baby in suspended Cochiti cradleboard, 1906.
Cradleboards were often put in swings or, in this case, suspended
from a tree or ceiling with ropes, to prevent harm from other
children or the bite of the red ant. Occasionally the mother would
give it a swing, and then continue on with her work undisturbed.

94. Interior of the Catholic mission church at Santo Domingo pueblo.

95. Interior of the Catholic mission church at Isleta pueblo.

96. Isleta pueblo.

97. Isleta, Catholic mission church in background.

*98. Two young pueblo women in front of Santo Domingo
Catholic mission church.*

BETWEEN SNAPSHOT AND DOCUMENT

Simeon Schwemberger's Photographs, 1902–8

Michele M. Penhall

Early Accounts

> I have not limited myself to learning the characteristics of the Indian and informing myself about their customs and practices, I have sought in these practices and customs, vestiges of the most remote antiquity.
> —FATHER JOSEPH FRANÇOIS LAFITAU, 1724[1]

Europeans have recorded the Indians of North America in images since the arrival of Christopher Columbus in the fifteenth century. Ranging from maps to renderings from travelogues, these images originally had limited public circulation.[2] By the eighteenth century a tradition of widely circulated graphic and painted images of Indians had evolved. This visual tradition was both continued and further popularized by the introduction of photography in the nineteenth century. The professionals and amateurs who photographed Native Americans followed conventions already established by artists in drawn, painted, and graphic works. Simeon Schwemberger was an amateur without formal training, but his photographs of Native Americans living in the Southwest are as sophisticated as the works of such better-known ethnographic photographers as J. K. Hillers, Charles Lummis, and Adam Clark Vroman. Revealing a kinship between photographer and subject that extends beyond ethnographic documentation,

Schwemberger's images also record important aspects of Native American culture, rituals, and architecture, while simultaneously suggesting a culturally foreign presence within reservation and pueblo life. Schwemberger's work provides an opportunity to examine not only customs peculiar to southwestern natives, but also, as Father Lafitau suggests, the European interest in the "vestiges of the most remote antiquity."

Before the advent of photography in 1839, artists and amateurs who traveled across North America documented its native inhabitants in many different ways. The Jesuit priest Father Joseph Lafitau spent five years, 1712–16, at Saint-Louis du Sault, an Iroquois settlement near Montreal, Canada; in 1724, his two-volume work, *Moeurs des Sauvages Ameriquains, Comparées aux Moeurs des Premiers Temps,* was published in Paris.[3] Along with elaborate descriptions of the Iroquois religion, trading policies, warfare strategies, ceremonies, mourning rituals, education, and marriage practices, Lafitau illustrated his text with many copper-plate engravings. Lafitau's work was the result of his direct experience with, and active participation in, the lives of the Indians he studied, but the images were stylized to suit western European conventions of composition and technique in an attempt to convey the Iroquois and Huron to an audience far removed from the Native American context.

The next stage in this history of representation is epitomized by the American artist George Catlin, who spent the years 1830–36 recording the Plains Indians, their daily activities, and views of the Plains landscape.[4] Catlin executed over 500 paintings, which were exhibited in an "Indian Gallery" that toured the United States and Europe. He also published, in 1841, an illustrated two-volume work entitled *Letters and Notes on the Manners, Customs, and Conditions of the North American Indians.* His exploration of Native American cultures and customs was rooted in contemporary romantic perceptions of the Indian that stressed the ethnographic local color of his life within the context of his environment.[5] More hostile and overtly racist opinions about Indians were held by many Anglos. Catlin himself felt that the Indians should be segregated in a designated area out West, yet his work recorded aspects of Native American life that would soon disappear in the face of relentless, pioneering expansion of European Americans.

In the spring of 1833, the German Prince Maximilian Philipp and the Swiss illustrator Karl Bodmer journeyed up the Missouri River.[6] Following a path similar to that taken by George Catlin, as well as Meriwether Lewis and William Clark in 1804–6, Prince Maximilian, an avid naturalist, and Bodmer, an aspiring artist, spent days and sometimes weeks among the Northwest Indians, paying close attention to native costumes, village life, and intertribal activities. While Maximilian collected artifacts and made extensive notes, Bodmer concentrated on field drawings of his subjects, at times spending several days on a single portrait to achieve what he considered to be an accurate likeness and a sense of the individual person.[7] In 1839, Maximilian published his research as the *Reise in das Innere Nord-America in den Jahre 1832 bis 1834,* which was translated into French in 1840–43 and into English in 1843. Bodmer's drawings and watercolors, transferred into a series of aquatints, were published separately between 1839 and 1841.[8]

Other artists such as Gustavus Hesselius (1682–1755), Charles Peale (1741–1827), Charles Bird King (1785–1862), and John Mix Stanley (1814–72) were among the individuals who recorded the native people of North America. While both the written accounts and the visual images are often culturally biased and factually incorrect, they remain valuable documents for two reasons. First, they preserve, however inaccurately, aspects of the rapidly changing, if not vanishing, native societies of North America. Second, these stylized images are insights into the preconceptions of the explorers, missionaries, and artists who documented North America's indigenous people.[9]

Photography was quickly recognized as an important documentary tool, and some expedition staffs included daguerreotypists. One of the first to join such an expedition was John Mix Stanley, a member of John Charles Frémont's expedition in the early 1850s to survey transcontinental railroad routes.[10] None of his daguerreotypes survive, but his earlier experience as a draughtsman reportedly contributed to his success as a photographer because it gave him a keen eye for details.[11] It became a matter of course to include photographers in all treks through the western territories, including the four major geological and ethnological expeditions of the nineteenth century: the King Survey of 1870–79, the Wheeler Survey of 1871–79, the Hayden Survey of 1870–79, and the Powell Survey of 1871–79. At least twenty-two different photographers worked in the Southwest between 1870 and 1900.[12] Many are familiar to us: J. K. Hillers, Timothy O'Sullivan, William Henry Jackson, Charles Lummis, and Edward S. Curtis. Others are less familar: G. Wharton James, Elizabeth Snyder, Orloff Westmann, Matilda Coxe Stevenson, Ben Wittick, William Bell, and James Mooney. By the beginning of the twentieth century, many of the major southwestern pueblos and reservations—Acoma, Tesuque, San Felipe, Santa Clara, Zuni, Santa Ana, Nambe, Taos, Laguna, Santo Domingo, Oraibi, and Walpi—had been visited and recorded by professional as well as amateur photographers.

Native Americans often had misgivings about photographers recording them and their ceremonies. But, such visual records could not exist without at least their partial consent and participation. Photographers often bartered or exchanged currency to photograph their subjects; indeed, as far back as the eighteenth century, artists had negotiated exchanges of goods and services to produce images of Native Americans. Some artists abused their artistic privilege to the point that Pueblo leaders imposed limits on photographers. In the case of the Hopi, all photography was banned soon after 1900.[13] Even today, photographing special native ceremonies and dances is not permitted on most pueblos and reservations. Still, the wealth of extant paintings, engravings, and photographs surviving in collections all over the world indicates that many artists negotiated and worked successfully with Indians; sources also suggest that Indians were often surprised by and fascinated with the results. Karl Bodmer's portraits so impressed the Mandan Indians that they gave him the nickname "Kawakpuska," which meant "the one who makes pictures."[14] The daguerreotypes of John Stanley were to his subjects, the Blackfeet, a combination of their sun worship with his photographic skill.[15] It is naive to believe that Native Americans were merely passive subjects before the illustrator's sketchbook or the photographer's lens, contributing nothing more than their appearance to the documentary process. Tacitly, but inevitably, the subject must have influenced the point of view, and the pictorial conventions, brought by the photographer. These photographs are neither simple representations, nor mirrors reflecting back on the author, but are instead windows looking in two directions at once.

Aided by the expansion of the Santa Fe Railroad, travelers could conveniently reach many pueblos located in the Southwest by the early 1880s. From 1895 to 1910, an entire generation of artists and photographers descended upon the Native Americans living in Arizona and New Mexico. Besides the ethnographic concerns of government agencies, the lucre of tourism attracted many artists and photographers to the Southwest. With the addition of Christian missionaries, who continued their work building schools and churches for the native population, the region was overrun by visitors traveling from pueblo to pueblo, and reservation to reservation. Vroman photographed at Zuni, Taos, Santa Clara, Pojoaque, and Santo Domingo in 1899; Curtis documented the pueblos at San Juan, Acoma, and San Ildefonso, and Santa Clara between 1904 and 1906; Jo Mora photographed the Hopi at Walpi and Sichomovi and the camp at Hotevilla in 1902–6.[16] Simeon Schwemberger belonged to this influx of ethnographers, tourists and missionaries.

The Amateur

Since manipulation of photographic composition occurs to a greater extent when the photographer is highly skilled (or when the photographer simply spends time thinking about his or her desired final image), photographs taken by amateurs may be more useful than images produced by professionals.
—ROBERT M. LEVINE[17]

In 1901 Simeon Schwemberger reached St. Michaels Mission, near Window Rock, Arizona, from Cincinnati. He was thirty-four years old and a lay brother in the Franciscan Order of Friars Minor. St. Michaels was founded in 1898 by three Franciscans, Brother Placid, Father Juvenal Schnorbus, and Father Anselm Weber, and their primary goal was to convert the natives to Catholicism and to construct schools to educate the Native American children. Within one year Schwemberger acquired a camera and began photographing the people he met and the places he visited. After seven years he abandoned his Franciscan calling and probably also his photographic avocation; he spent the next twenty-three years, until his death in 1931, involved in a variety of enterprises that included the task of printing his approximately 400 negatives.

Schwemberger had no formal training as an artist, and the question of his originality is not at issue here. There was already a rich tradition of representing Native American cultures when photographers began documenting the western frontier and its indigenous people. Amateur and professional photographers alike extended this tradition: Schwemberger's work is an important thread in the fabric of that pictorial legacy. The importance of his photographs lies not in any one particular image, but in his work as a whole. Like a written journal, Schwemberger's pictures form a diary of his experiences during his tenure at St. Michaels. His portraits constitute more than a catalogue of ethnographic types—they are an extension of the visual tradition of Native American images established by professional and amateur artists since the fifteenth century.

Schwemberger's primary duties at St. Michaels included all of the household domestic chores—cooking, cleaning, and maintaining the lodgings and the school house. He took special pride in the mission's garden, which was an important resource for St. Michaels residents. The portrait in Figure 1 has Schwemberger posed as the photographer, next to a 5 x 7 Burke and James box camera supported on a wooden tripod. His scruffy appearance and well-worn cardigan are made irrelevant by his introspective, contemplative gaze. Another portrait, possibly taken by a fellow brother, shows Brother Simeon standing in a field of young corn among his gardening tools, dressed in rumpled work clothes and dust-covered shoes (Fig. 2). While these staged images lack spontaneity, they record Schwemberger's complementary roles of lay brother and photographer, of the laborer and the artist.

Professional artists often came only to record special ceremonies and prominent individuals before traveling on to other sites. Rituals like the Hopi Snake Dance, which is just one dance in their annual cycle, were documented extensively, but in isolation from the more continuous ritual fabric of Hopi life. It was usually the amateur who, working over extended periods in the region where he lived, pho-

99. Karl Bodmer (Swiss, 1809–93), Mácchsi-Karéhde, Mandan Man.

tographed the routine, daily dimensions of the indigenous cultures. Schwemberger spent seven years, 1902–8, photographing the Navajo, Hopi, and Pueblo peoples, ceremonies, dances, and architecture of Arizona and New Mexico. He also recorded the many workers and visitors to St. Michaels Mission. Since Schwemberger's early training was religious rather than artistic, his photographic education was acquired largely through direct experience. The many photographers traveling throughout the area at the turn of the century and the large numbers of photographs in circulation and available at major trading posts in the Southwest may indirectly have furthered Schwemberger's artistic education. It was through this eclectic mixture of experience and exposure to ethnographers, photographers, and collections of photographs that Simeon Schwemberger gained his knowledge.

100. Santo Domingo man, Santo Domingo pueblo, New Mexico, 1906.

Although Schwemberger was an amateur, many of his photographs reflect an awareness of established pictorial conventions. The photograph he made in 1906 of a Santo Domingo native is analogous to Karl Bodmer's portrait of Plains Indian Máhchsi-Karéhde, executed seventy years earlier (Figs. 99, 100). Máhchsi-Karéhde was an important tribal leader whom Bodmer portrayed dressed in all of his finery. Schwemberger's subject, a Santo Domingo man, stands in front of the Catholic church, draped in a much simpler blanket, but with the same heroic pose and the same intense gaze that Bodmer used in his watercolor. Also at Santo Domingo, Schwemberger photographed two young women in the same setting, in the same manner, with the same heroic stance (Fig. 98).

Schwemberger frequently used a three-quarter profile view when photographing individuals. Three portraits of a young Cochiti woman, a young Navajo boy, and a Navajo man named Jake are examples (Figs. 101–3). The three-quarter view, a standard portrait device that dates back to the Renaissance, was popular with both painters and photographers. Each of these images has an obvious ethnographic interest in the details of the subjects' costume and jewelry. More important, however, is the sense of individuality projected by the glance that is directed, not at the photographer, but rather at a psychological space defined by each subject. One sees a gentle yet nervous girl who looks past the man photographing her. The young boy and the man, Jake, photographed in the same location assume identical poses. Seen here together Jake appears as the young boy's ideal grown-up, with the same clenched jaw but now with a sadness in his eyes. Equivalently, Schwemberger's portrait of Hastiin Becheii Ba'a d transferred this pictorial convention from the out-of-doors to a studio-like setting (Fig. 104). Placed before a neutral backdrop, the Navajo woman sits in three-quarter profile. Her gaze, directed away from the photographer's lens, is clear and deliber-

101. Rosaria, a Cochiti Indian, 1906.

COPYRIGHT 1907 BY
SIMEON SCHWEMBERGER

102. Young Navajo boy, 1907.

103. Jake, a Navajo man, 1907.
Paul Long notes that he is in turn–of–the–century traditional cloth–
ing of a brightly colored headband, Pendleton blanket, and squash
blossom necklace.

104. Hastiin Becheii Ba'aa d. Navajo matron.

105. A gathering of friends on Sunday.
Paul Long notes that this photograph was taken in front of the first
mission at St. Michaels. Left to right, Hans Funk, Anna Funk,
Anselm Weber, Bonina, and his family. Ninth from left is Father
Berard Haile. Anna B. Day and Sam E. Day are third and fourth
from right.

ate, her posture erect. This portrait achieves a balance between romantic idealization and scientific documentation.

Despite his awareness of various pictorial conventions,
Schwemberger did not always photograph his subjects with a
consistent concern for formal expression. A group portrait
of St. Michaels residents dressed in their Sunday best is revealing (Fig. 105). A more professional photographer might
have centered this group before the mission building, but
Schwemberger placed them toward one side, with the result
that the building's corner rises awkwardly out of Father An-

106. Dinner in the desert.
Paul Long notes: W. E. Hildebrand, Schwemberger, Elizabeth Funk, and an unidentified woman enjoy a picnic near Oraibi.

selm Weber's head. Yet the group is balanced symmetrically to either side of the central woman in white. Another photograph records a picnic near Oraibi with Schwemberger, W. E. Hildebrand (a contractor working at St. Michaels), Elizabeth Funk, and an unidentified woman (Fig. 106). Schwemberger carefully framed this scene and positioned himself in the center of the group. His glance towards the lens indicates that he was himself self-consciously aware of the camera. Even so, he photographed the outing without bothering either to clean up the foreground with its empty tin cans or to direct the other three figures. The result is an informal vignette of a casual event. Schwemberger used a similarly informal approach in his photograph of Mrs. Whitegoat at St. Michaels

107. Mrs. Whitegoat, Navajo, St. Michaels, ca. 1906.

(Fig. 107). The effect is both intimate and accidental, as if the photographer had interrupted Mrs. Whitegoat and the nuzzling horse.

Like many other photographers of the Southwest, Simeon Schwemberger photographed scenes of Native American life that fit the conventions of European genre images. One popular type was the image of a Pueblo woman with a pot, a

*108. Adam Clark Vroman, Woman of Isleta
with Olla on her Head, 1899.*

109. A girl of Cochiti, 1906.

basket, or a weaving in progress (Figs. 108, 109). Vroman's photograph made in 1899 shows a woman from Isleta, and Schwemberger's image from 1906 depicts a young girl from Cochiti. Both are dressed in ceremonial garments, wearing jewelry and woven shawls, and each balances a clay pot on her head. The difference between these photographs is found not in the figures, but in their context. Vroman has placed his subject in a pristine setting, largely free from visual distractions, so that the woman acts as the sole focus of attention. Vroman used the adobe wall as a photographer would use a neutral backdrop in a studio. Conversely, Schwemberger placed his subject against a more cluttered background that gives the viewer a glimpse of the real environment of the pueblo. The pots scattered along the back wall, the puppy sitting near the doorway, and the late afternoon shadows across the ground are distractions that compete for attention yet suggest the daily atmosphere of the young girl's life.

Another genre, the "madonna and child," further specifies the similarities and the differences between a professional photographer like Vroman and an amateur like Schwemberger. The subject for Vroman's 1901 image is a young Hopi mother seated in a doorway nursing her young child (Fig. 110). Propped up beside her are two woven trays that are used in sacred ceremonies.[18] These trays were added to the setting by Vroman perhaps to enhance the cultural exoticism of the image.[19] Schwemberger's photograph, made five years later, shows another Hopi mother with her child suckling at her breast (Fig. 111). To her left rests the child's fur-lined cradleboard and to her right, a walking stick. Whereas the area around Vroman's subject is virtually free of distracting elements except the carefully placed ceremonial trays, Schwemberger left in place the clutter of wood scraps and other debris that surround his subject. If the cradle and walking stick were introduced for effect, they are at least immediately relevant to the mother and child and are not simply

110. *Adam Clark Vroman,* Hopi Woman
and Child at Mishongnovi, *1901.*

111. *Simeon Schwemberger,*
Hopi Madonna, *1906.*

decorative props. Vroman's placement of the trays and the
uncluttered area around his subject suggests his more deliber-
ate attempt to construct a pictorial balance in his pictures.
Schwemberger chose instead to record the same scene in its
more natural and accidental state.

Schwemberger also photographed some of the Americans
who reshaped and, in some cases, preserved the Southwest.
On a Sunday in 1905 he photographed seven soldiers in front
of a supply tent, at Fort Defiance, Arizona (Fig. 112). The
soldier's disheveled uniforms and the muddy setting are less
than picturesque, but with the sole exception of the third
from the right, all the men were obviously pleased with being
photographed. The two men in the center, would–be Teddy

112. Sunday in Fort Defiance, 1905.

Paul Long notes that Fort Defiance was first occupied by American troops in September 1851 as a post for operations against the Navajo. In April 1861 troops were withdrawn from the fort to take part in the Civil War. In 1868 Fort Defiance was chosen as the site for the Navajo Indian Agency. The first government school for the Navajo was established at the fort in 1870. In June of 1890 the agency was transferred to military control.

Roosevelts, have struck particularly jaunty poses. The anthropologist Stewart Culin struck an equally jaunty and dramatic pose for Schwemberger around 1905–6 (Fig. 3). Culin spent his summers in the Southwest collecting Indian artifacts that he left, along with his notebooks, to the Brooklyn Museum. Here he plays the quintessential frontier man—armed

113. John Foley and collection.

with a rifle and a revolver, holding a cigar in his left hand, he stands on an impromptu stage created from some of his treasures: two Navajo blankets and an animal skin. The theatrical and artificial quality of this portrait is in marked contrast to the relative informality of Schwemberger's portraits of Native Americans.

An even greater exhibit of Indian artifacts than Cullin's display is Schwemberger's photograph which he titled *John Foley and Collection* (Fig. 113). Foley, shown here leaning against a post with a pipe in his mouth, looks past the photographer with a cynical stare. From this image, we see that he has amassed a large collection of contemporary and prehistoric artifacts; he will no doubt profit from their sale.

The Anasazi pieces and the two skulls are especially grim and sad reminders of the unsanctioned excavations which took place across the territory, largely for personal gain. Another image by Schwemberger depicts precisely the western objects and clothing that replaced the native tools and garments lost by Native Americans. His look inside J. B. Moore's Crystal Trading Post, in Crystal, New Mexico, reveals a collection of hats, gloves, scarves, bolts of fabric, tack, and cooking utensils—familiar items to westerners but not necessarily to natives of the Southwest (Fig. 5). Yet these are the items for sale to the general public which included Native Americans. This replacement of articles from one culture to another is further emphasized by the three Indians standing at the counter. With their backs to the camera, it is clear by their Western clothes that their more native style of dress has also been replaced.

Schwemberger's eight-year tenure at St. Michaels acquainted him personally with many Indians and permitted him to capture the dualities in Native American culture. A photograph of two Navajo war chiefs, standing side by side, illustrates the effect of European acculturation (Fig. 114). On the left is Bi-lee-kla-Zhin, who is dressed in Western attire: pin-striped pants, button vest, knotted kerchief, a felt hat, holster with several bullets, and a revolver that is visible under his left arm. He wears only three Navajo articles: a blanket draped over his shoulders, a beaded necklace, and a native belt buckle. Next to him stands Taiyoni, who conceals his store-bought shirt and jacket beneath a Navajo blanket. Instead of a cowboy hat, he wears a headband. Tai-o-ne presents himself to the photographer in a more traditional style.

This issue of acculturation is emphasized again in Schwemberger's portrait of a Keres Indian couple from Cochiti (Fig. 115). The young woman, Rosaria, is shown in full ceremonial dress, complete with leggings, moccasins, and elaborate sil-

114. *Old Navajo war chiefs, "Bi-lee-Kla-Zhin"*
(Black Horse) on the left and Taiyoni.

115. Rosaria and José, Keres Indians, Cochiti, New Mexico, 1906.

ver and bead jewelry, and her face is painted. The man, José, wears a brimmed hat, pullover shirt, and trousers tucked into his hightop boots. But acculturation involves more than one's choice of clothing. While the Navajo chiefs at least retained their native names, this Cochiti couple is identified by the Spanish and Christian names of Rosaria and José. The strong Catholic presence throughout the reservations and pueblos is suggested in another photograph, this time of a father who is seated with two of his sons on the steps of St. Michaels Mission, while an older son stands alongside (Fig. 116). The father and elder son wear moccasins and Navajo jewelry and have partly retained their native style of dress, but the youngest boys have not. Their hair cropped short, clothed in parochial school uniforms, knitted stockings, and lace-up boots, they testify to the acculturation the missionaries often required of the indigenous people.

Schwemberger also photographed the architecture of the Southwest. Two views taken in 1906 of the Keresan village of Cochiti and the Hopi village of Oraibi are representative (Figs. 117, 118). Both try to capture a sense of the pueblo as a whole and in relationship to the site. Schwemberger's dramatic view of Oraibi is taken from below to emphasize the large desert expanse that rises up to the pueblo, and the threatening clouds above that take up half of the picture frame. This photograph suggests the harmony of a culture whose architecture was a natural extension of the land and which existed in a delicate balance between the contrasting forces of earth and sky. The concern for architectural composition is seen as well in two detail views of Oraibi made in 1906 (Figs. 119, 120), which show both Schwemberger's eye for the anecdotal circumstance and his awareness of the fragility of the earth and stone structures. Lines across the bottom of each plate indicate his subsequent intention to crop images. It is likely that these crop lines were intended for the prints he sold later in his commercial business: Schwemberger con-

116. Navajo men and children, St. Michaels, ca. 1906.
Paul Long notes that the two small children are wearing their
school uniforms while the older men are in the more traditional
dress of the time.

117. Cochiti pueblo.

118. Oraibi, 1906.

119. Oraibi, 1906.

120. Oraibi, 1906.

121. Lean-to shade, 1906.
Paul Long notes that this structure fits the description of a "two-legged single lean-to" from Jett and Spencer, *Navajo Architecture.*

tinued to print his negatives after he left St. Michaels, in 1909, which he sold either individually as postcards or assembled together in albums.

Schwemberger also recorded the domestic architecture of the more nomadic Navajos. In each photograph Schwemberger caught a different kind of view of a Navajo family in relation to their home—from the ethnographic portrait of a family lined up in front of their "lean-to shade" (Fig. 121), to a more candid shot of a family clustered outside a similar "lean-to shade" (Fig. 122), to a contextual view of four Navajos and their hogan and ramada near the bottom of Canyon de Chelly

122. A Navajo one-legged double lean-to shade.
Paul Long notes that Jett and Spencer record these structures as
having no differentiation between roof and walls. They were constructed of posts leaned against a single ridge pole. These shades
have been associated with the early Navajo archaeology of the
eighteenth century.

(Fig. 123). Aside from the architectural importance of these
photographs, the images portray different levels of intimacy
within each family group.

In his travels for St. Michaels, Schwemberger also documented the region's Spanish Colonial Mission churches. His
view of the church at Isleta is competent, conventional, and
also curiously different in character from his photographs of
Native American architecture (Fig. 124). Whereas those photographs sought to contextualize the architecture either in

123. Sub-rectangular "Four-legged or leaning log hogan,"
Canyon deChelly.

Paul Long notes that in the late 1800s the leaning-log hogan was uncommon. The conical hogan was more popular. The leaning-log hogan was used more during the twentieth century because of the large living space available. On the left is a flat-roofed shade or ramada. The simplest form of the flat-roofed shade consists of poles supported by stringers placed between four vertical posts as illustrated in this photograph.

124. The Catholic mission church at Isleta.

terms of its site or in terms of the life of its inhabitants, this view of the Isleta church excludes any sense of its site or of the people it served. The church rises up as an abstract object in an equally abstract void, as if somehow divorced from the local culture. Other photographs such as two interior views of the churches of Cochiti and Santo Domingo taken around 1906, focus on the Spanish Colonial religious paintings and sculptures (Figs. 83, 95). To the Franciscans for whom Schwemberger worked, these photographs were evidence of the success of the Catholic church in converting the Native American peoples of the Southwest. For those Native Americans, the churches built in pueblos and on reservations

125. Oraibi, 1906.

signaled an irrevocable change in their spiritual beliefs and practices.[20]

Schwemberger's amateur style resulted in, at times, candid views such as the image made at Oraibi in 1906 (Fig. 125). Somewhere between a snapshot and an ethnographic document, this photograph records both the Hopi at home in their pueblo and the presence of tourists, who, now more than ever, were a dominant force in Native American lives. The three figures standing between the adobe structures are the same individuals seen picnicing with Schwemberger in an earlier image (see Fig. 106). These photographs reminded Schwemberger and the people of St. Michaels of specific

*126. "The Laughing Doctor" at Day's chicken pull,
St. Michaels, August 10, 1905.*

characters or a particular day's activities, and for subsequent
audiences the pictures function as historical records of per-
sonalities and events that have passed. Information gleaned
from Schwemberger's images is an essential link in understanding the pioneer settlements in the Southwest and their
effect on Native American culture.

Two other images by Schwemberger, *The Laughing Doctor
at Day's Chicken Pulling* and a photograph of four participants
in that event, present his more candid style (Figs. 126, 127).
Although Kodak introduced hand-held cameras in the late
1880s, Schwemberger continued to use his 5x7 box camera
on a tripod. Thus, it is to his credit that many of his photo-

127. Chicken Pull, St. Michaels, ca. 1905.

graphs reflect some degree of spontaneity. These two specific images are from Schwemberger's extensive documentation of the Nightway Chant, the Navajo healing ceremonial he recorded in 1905 near St. Michaels. Charles Day financed this event and obtained photographic access for Schwemberger.[21] He photographed the sacred and temporal aspects of the nine-day ceremony, including the sandpaintings, masked impersonators, and the chicken pull.[22] Published here for the first time, Schwemberger's account represents one of the few complete visual and written descriptions of this important Navajo ceremony, and his contribution is significant to the understanding of the ritual.

In his portrait of the artist Herbert Judy at Red Rock in

128. Mr. Herbert B. Judy, artist at Red Rock, ca. 1904.
Paul Long notes that Judy was hired by the Hubbells to make a colored illustration of one of the Navajo rugs in their collection.

129. Window Rock, Arizona.

1904, Schwemberger reveals the degree to which he was ultimately aware of the larger function of his photographs: by showing Judy without showing what Judy is sketching, Schwemberger identifies the artist not simply as the recorder of impressions but more essentially as the intermediary between the object and its audience (Fig. 128). Schwemberger's photographic documents thus recreate for us the world as *he* saw it. The photograph he took of Window Rock toward the end of his career in 1908 suggests that he interpreted that world as the juxtaposition of two cultures in an often memorable natural setting: at the base of the cliff face a Navajo dwelling represents the indigenous Native American; the sin-

187

gle tourist standing in the voided eye of Window Rock itself represents the colonizing European (Fig. 129).

> In the present as in the past, to understand the Indian is
> to understand an "other" according to one's own culture.
> ROBERT BERKHOFER[23]

Since most outside efforts to comprehend a foreign culture are influenced by the perspectives of one's own culture, so too was Schwemberger's understanding of Native Americans filtered through his religious and secular training and beliefs. Like his predecessors and contemporaries, he approached his subjects from the perspective of an outsider. But even if his pictures are the biased and fragmentary record of a rich and extensive civilization, they are, nevertheless, important vestiges of a past that no longer exists.

NOTES

The Hubbell Papers and the St. Michaels Collection are housed in the Special Collections Library of the University of Arizona in Tucson.

Introduction

1. Wilken, Robert L. *Anselm Weber, O.F.M. Missionary to the Navaho* (Milwaukee: Bruce Publishing Co. 1955), pp. vii–x. The Anselm Weber.
2. Ibid.
3. Ibid. p. 8.
4. Ibid., p. 9.
5. Washington Matthews to A. Weber, October 1, 1898, in Wilken, *Anselm Weber, O.F.M.,* p. 38.

The Early Years

1. Wilken, *Anselm Weber, O.F.M.,* p. 85.
2. Ibid., p. 95.
3. Ibid., p. 94.
4. Ibid.

5. Ibid.

6. Ibid.

7. Ibid.

8. Ibid., pp. 103–4.

9. St. Michaels House Financial Records, 1901–28, Box 11, St. Michaels Collection.

10. A. Weber to Charles Lusk, November 4, 1913, St. Michaels Collection.

11. St. Michaels House Financial Records, 1901–28, Box 11 and Box 55.

12. S. Schwemberger to Stewart Culin, February 25, 1906, Stewart Culin Archival Collection, Brooklyn Museum, Brooklyn, New York.

13. S. Schwemberger to J. L. Hubbell, April 27, 1906, St. Michaels Collection.

14. A. Weber to the Father Provincial, July 13, 1904, St. Michaels Collection.

15. A. Weber to the Father Provincial, July 13, 1904, St. Michaels Collection.

16. A. Weber to the Father Provincial, July 13, 1904. St. Michaels Collection.

17. S. Schwemberger to Stewart Culin, February 25, 1906, Stewart Culin Archival Collection.

18. *McKinley County Republican,* December 9, 1905.

19. S. Schwemberger to Stewart Culin, February 25, 1906, Stewart Culin Archival Collection.

20. Stewart Culin expedition report, June 17, 1909, Stewart Culin Archival Collection.

The Florida Connection

1. Camp Willard consisted of seventy acres of land, six miles east of Largo, Florida, near the confluence of Cross Bayou and Tampa Bay. The fundamental idea of the winter resort was to make it something different from the fine hotels already in operation in Florida. The brothers' intent was to develop a place where people could come to enjoy nature. To this end the resort was successful.

This particular piece of land is near the present St. Petersburg–Clearwater International airport. *Pinellas Counselor,* May 11, 1911.

2. S. Schwemberger to Sharlot Hall, February 19, 1911. *Sharlot Hall Museum,* Box 1, File folder 5, Item 1a.

3. Ibid.

4. Ibid.

5. Cedar Springs Trading Post was built in the 1880s by Jake Tobin, one of the first traders to settle in the valley south of the Hopi Mesas. Frank McNitt, *The Indian Traders* (Norman: University of Oklahoma Press, 1962), p. 204.

The Indian Trader

1. John and Lillian Theobold, *Arizona Territorial Post Offices and Postmasters* (Phoenix: Arizona Historical Foundation, 1961), p. 90.

2. S. Schwemberger to J. L. Hubbell, September 13, 1911, Hubbell Papers.

Ibid.

3. S. Schwemberger to Roman Hubbell, December 12, 1911, Hubbell Papers.

4. S. Schwemberger to Roman Hubbell, February 29, 1912, Hubbell Papers.

5. Ibid.

6. Ibid.

7. S. Schwemberger to Roman Hubbell, March 2, 1912, Hubbell Papers.

8. Ibid.

9. The decade beginning in 1910 saw a decline in the production of quality Navajo rugs expressly due to the introduction by the government of French Rambouilett sheep. With this new breed the government hoped to increase the production of mutton for the Navajo. In that regard it was successful, but the fleece produced was oily and extremely difficult to clean, card, spin, and weave. Consequently, the rugs were heavy, coarse, and generally of inferior quality. In order to stimulate the continued production of rugs, the traders began to buy the rugs by the pound: thus the "pound rug" evolved. In order to increase the weight of the rugs

the weavers wove the wool without removing the grease and dirt, thereby making them heavier. Not until the 1940s was this devastating trend curbed and fine Navajo weaving revived. H. L. James, *Rugs and Posts* (West Chester, Pa.: Schiffer Publishing, 1988), p. 14.

10. S. Schwemberger to Roman Hubbell, March 28, 1912, Hubbell Papers.

11. S. Schwemberger to Roman Hubbell, April 15, 1912, Hubbell Papers.

12. S. Schwemberger to Postmaster, Ganado, Arizona, August 13, 1912, Hubbell Papers.

13. Ibid.

14. S. Schwemberger to J. L. Hubbell, August 29, 1912, Hubbell Papers.

15. S. Schwemberger to J. L. Hubbell, September 5, 1912, Hubbell Papers.

16. Ibid.

17. S. Schwemberger to J. L. Hubbell, September 9, 1912, Hubbell Papers.

18. Ibid.

19. S. Schwemberger to J. L. Hubbell, September 11, 1912, Hubbell Papers.

20. S. Schwemberger to J. L. Hubbell, September 9, 1912, Hubbell Papers.

21. A. Weber to Charles Lusk, November 4, 1913, St. Michaels Papers.

22. Records of McKinley County, Marriage License No. 402, McKinley County Court House, Gallup, New Mexico.

23. S. Schwemberger to J. L. Hubbell, September 29, 1912, Hubbell Papers.

24. A. Weber to Charles Lusk, November 4, 1913, St. Michaels Papers.

25. C. C. Manning to A. Weber, August 26, 1913, St. Michaels Papers.

26. Joel Higgins McAdams came to Arizona in 1895. He worked at Red Lake and Tuba City until the Spanish American War in 1898. He enlisted in the Rough Riders. After the war he owned a trading store in Chaves, New Mexico. In 1907, in partnership with Edwin

Jacob Marty, he build the Sunrise Springs Trading Post and subsequently bought Indian Wells and another post at Keams Canyon. He bought out Marty and in 1909 sold Sunrise Springs to Hubert Richardson. McAdams stayed at Indian Wells. In 1910 he sold Indian Wells to Richardson and opened a post north of the tracks in Gallup. In 1918 he sold his company to John Kirk. John McNitt, *The Indian Traders,* pp. 273–74.

27. S. Schwemberger to J. L. Hubbell, October 1913, St. Michaels Papers.

28. A. Weber to C. Lusk, November 4, 1913, St. Michaels Papers.

29. S. Schwemberger to J. L. Hubbell, December 5, 1913, Hubbell Papers.

30. S. Schwemberger to J. L. Hubbell, December 27, 1913, Hubbell Papers.

31. S. Schwemberger to J. L. Hubbell, April 23, 1914, Hubbell Papers.

32. S. Schwemberger to J. L. Hubbell, February 13, 1915, Hubbell Papers.

33. *Gallup Independent,* November 9, 1916.

34. McKinley County District Court, Case Number 1082, February 18, 1919, Gallup, New Mexico.

35. *Gallup Independent,* June 26, 1919.

36. Business Directory of Gallup and McKinley County, 1920.

37. *Gallup Independent,* November 4, 1920.

38. Personal communication with Eunice Fellin, July 1988.

39. Personal communication with Eunice Fellin, July 1988.

40. Personal communication with Eunice Fellin, July 1988.

41. *Gallup Independent,* March 11, 1930.

42. Personal communication with Eunice Fellin, July 1988.

43. *Gallup Independent,* January 23, 1931.

The Odyssey

1. Peter Havens, personal interview with author, Gallup, New Mexico, July 18, 1967.

2. Carmen Charimonte, personal interview with author, Gallup, New Mexico, July 1967.

3. Peter Havens, personal interview with author, Gallup, New Mexico, July 1967.

4. Ibid.

5. John B. Moore, *The Navajo* (Denver: The William-Haffner Co., 1911).

The Nightway

The Night Chant is rich in symbolism which is not adequately discussed in Schwemberger's account; however it is not the purpose of this book to delve into the intricacies of the ceremony. The following volumes are listed to direct the reader to a more thorough and knowledgeable discussion of the Nightway ceremony.

Faris, James C. *The Nightway: A History and A History of Documentation of a Navajo Ceremonial,* Albuquerque: University of New Mexico Press, 1990.

Matthews, Washington. *The Night Chant, A Navajo Ceremony.* Memoirs of the American Museum of Natural History, vol. 6. New York: Knickerbocker Press, 1902.

Newcomb, Franc Johnson, Stanley Fishler, and Mary C. Wheelwright. *A Study of Navajo Symbolism,* Papers of the Peabody Museum of Archaeology and Ethnology, vol. 32, no. 3. Cambridge, Mass.: Harvard University, 1956.

Wyman, Leland C. *Southwest Indian Drypainting.* Santa Fe and Albuquerque: School of American Research and University of New Mexico Press, 1983.

Acknowledgments: I wish to thank Dana Asbury for the opportunity to write this essay; and Eugenia Parry Janis, Christopher Mead, and Joyce Szabo for their insightful comments.

1. *Customs of the American Indians Compared with the Customs of Primitive Times by Father Joseph François Lafitau,* edited and translated by William Fenton and Elizabeth Moore (Toronto: Champlain Society, 1974) p. 27.

2. Robert F. Berkhofer, Jr., "White Conceptions of Indians" in *Handbook of North American Indians-History of Indian-White Relations,* Wilcomb Washburn, editor, (Washington D.C.: Smithsonian Institution, 1988), pp. 522–47.

3. Fenton and Moore, *Customs of the American Indians,* pp. xxxiii–xxxv.

4. John Wilmerding, *American Art* (New York: Penguin Books, 1976), p. 125.

5. Matthew Baigell, *A Concise History of American Painting and Sculpture* (New York: Harper and Row, 1984), p. 103.

6. John Ewers, *Views of a Vanishing Frontier* (Omaha: Center for Western Studies/Joslyn Art Museum, 1984), p. 10.

7. Ibid., p. 52.

8. Ibid., p. 47.

9. Patricia Trenton and Patrick Houlihan, *Native Americans-Five Centuries of Changing Images* (New York: Harry Abrams, 1989), p. 7.

10. Richard Rudisill, *Mirror Image* (Albuquerque: University of New Mexico Press, 1971), p. 107.

11. Ibid.

12. Alfonso Ortig, ed., *Handbook of North American Indians-Southwest* (Washington, D.C.: Smithsonian Institution, 1979), passim.

13. Ibid., p. 192.

14. Ewers, *Views of a Vanishing Frontier,* p. 80.

15. Rudisill, *Mirror Image,* p. 107.

16. Ortig, *Handbook of North American Indians.*

17. Robert Levine, *Images of History* (Durham: Duke University Press, 1989), p. x.

18. William Webb and Robert Weinstein, *Dwellers at the Source* (Albuquerque: University of New Mexico Press, 1987), p. 32.

19. Ibid.

20. Sherburne F. Cook and Cesare Marino, "Roman Catholic Missions and the Southwest" in *Handbook of North American Indians-History of Indian-White Relations,* Wilcomb Washburn, editor, (Washington D.C.: Smithsonian Institution, 1988), p. 479.

21. James C. Faris, *The Nightway: A History and a History of Documentation of a Navajo Ceremonial* (Albuquerque: University of New Mexico Press, 1990), p. 48.

22. Ibid.

23. Berkhofer, *Handbook of North American Indians,* p. 547.

THE SOURCES
OF THE PHOTOGRAPHS

The photographs for reproduction in this book were obtained from several sources. The list below indicates the institutions that kindly gave permission to use photographs from their collections for reproduction in this volume. The majority of the plates reproduced are contact prints, made on silver chloride paper from the original 5 x 7 glass-plate negatives. The remaining plates were produced from copy negatives from Schwemberger's original prints. For these no glass-plate negatives were found. The numbers preceded by SM refer to the St. Michaels Collection of the Franciscan Fathers at St. Michaels. Listed below are the letter designations for the other collections from which the photographs have been obtained.

SHM   Collections of Sharlot Hall Museum, Prescott, Arizona.

NPSG   Archives of the National Park Service, Hubbell Trading Post National Monument, Ganado, Arizona.

BMACAC   The Brooklyn Museum Archives, Stewart Culin Archival Collection.

MNA ms   Museum of Northern Arizona.

1. BMACAC. Expedition Report of 1907.
2. BMACAC. Expedition Report of 1905.
3. SM 1600.
4. BMACAC. Expedition Report of 1905.
5. MNA ms 168-6-29.
6. MNA ms 168-6-46.

7. MNA ms 168-6-45.

8. SM 1583.

9. SM 87.

10. SM 88.

11. SM 90.

12. SM 93.

13. NPSG 5504.

14. SHM.

15. NPSG.

16. MNA ms 168-2-3.

17. MNA ms 168-2-4.

18. SM 96.

19. SM 98.

20. NPSG 5511.

21. NPSG 5512.

22. SM 94.

23. MNA ms 168-2-7.

24. SHM.

25. SHM 25.

26. SM 100.

27. SM 99.

28. SM 97.

29. SM 102.

30. SM 522.

31. SM 763.

32. SM 81.

33. NPSG 5486.

34. NPSG 5377.

35. BMACAC. Expedition Report of 1906.

36. BMACAC. Expedition Report of 1907.

37. BMACAC. Expedition Report of 1907.

38. SM 1626.

39. SM 1541.

40. SM 1610.

41. SM 1588.

42. BMACAC. Expedition Report of 1907.

43. BMACAC. Expedition Report of 1907.

44. BMACAC. Expedition Report of 1907.
45. BMACAC. Expedition Report of 1907.
46. MNA ms 168-6-20.
47. SM 1629.
48. SM 250.
49. BMACAC. Expedition Report of 1906.
50. SM 39.
50. BMACAC. Expedition Report of 1906.
51. SHM.
52. SM 1771-296.
53. BMACAC. Expedition Report of 1907.
54. BMACAC. Expedition Report of 1906.
55. SM 256.
56. BMACAC. Expedition Report of 1907.
57. SM 666.
58. MNA ms 168-2-8.
59. SM 310.
60. MNA ms 168-2-24.
61. SM 1635.
62. SM 1625.
63. NPSG 5531.
64. SM 37.
65. SM 640.
66. SM 1547.
67. SM 70.
68. SM 1545.
69. SM 1556.
70. SM 1578.
71. SM 1539.
72. SM 1564.
73. SM 69.
74. SM 67.
75. SM 1543.
76. SM 1530.
77. SM 1528.
78. SM 45.

79. SM 43.

80. SM 1618.

81. SM 1554.

82. SM 77.

83. SM 1580.

84. SM 1896.

85. SM 71.

86. BMACAC. Expedition Report of 1907

87. BMACAC. Expedition Report of 1907

88. BMACAC. Expedition Report of 1907.

89. SM 1521.

90. SM 1538.

91. BMACAC. Expedition Report of 1907.

92. SM 1590.

93. SM 306.

94. SM 1631.

95. SM 1529.

96. SM 1548.

97. SM 1647.

98. SM 1574.

99. Watercolor and pencil, 16⅞ x 12 in., Joslyn Art Museum, Omaha, Nebraska.

100. SM 1519.

101. BMACAC. Expedition Report of 1907.

102. BMACAC.

103. BMACAC. Expedition Report of 1906.

104. NPSG 5532.

105. SM 827.

106. NPSG 5487.

107. SM 1540.

108. Seaver Center for Western History Research, Los Angeles County Museum of Natural History, no. V-1071.

109. BMACAC. Expedition Report of 1907.

110. Southwest Museum, Los Angeles, no. 20692.

111. SM 1610.

112. SM 20.

113. SM 1637.

114. SHM.

115. BMACAC. Expedition Report of 1907.

116. SM 1582.

117. SM 73.

118. SM 1655.

119. SM 1627.

120. SM 1646.

121. MNA ms 168-2-16.

122. SM 258.

123. SM 38.

124. SM 1535.

125. SM 1656.

126. BMACAC. Expedition Report of 1905.

127. NPSG 5452.

128. SM 1628.

129. MNA ms 168-6-40.

SELECTED BIBLIOGRAPHY

Ewers, John C. *Views of a Vanishing Frontier*. Omaha: Center for Western Studies/Joslyn Art Museum, 1984.

Fleming, Paula Richardson, and Judith Luskey. *The North American Indians in Early Photographs*. New York: Harper and Row, 1986.

Hathaway, Nancy. *Native American Portraits 1862–1918*. San Francisco: Chronicle Books, 1990.

McRae, William. "Images of Native Americans in Still Photography." *History of Photography* 13 (1989): 321–42.

Moneta, Daniela P., ed. *Charles F. Lummis—The Centennial Exhibition*. Los Angeles: Southwest Museum, 1985.

Nabokov, Peter, and Robert Easton. *Native American Architecture*. New York: Oxford University Press, 1989.

Ortiz, Alfonso, ed. *Handbook of North American Indians—Southwest*. Washington, D.C.: Smithsonian Institution Press, 1979.

Rudisill, Richard. *Mirror Image*. Albuquerque: University of New Mexico Press, 1971.

————. *Photographers of the New Mexico Territory 1845–1912*. Santa Fe: Museum of New Mexico Press, 1973.

Scherer, Joanna Cohan. "You can't believe your eyes: Inaccuracies in photographs of North American Indians." *Studies in the Anthropology of Visual Communication* 2 (1975): 67–79.

Trenton, Patricia, and Patrick Houlihan. *Native Americans—Five Centuries of Changing Images*. New York: Harry Abrams, 1989.

Webb, William, and Robert Weinstein. *Dwellers at the Source*. Albuquerque: University of New Mexico Press, 1987.

Wilken, Robert L. *Anselm Weber, O.F.M. Missionary to the Navajo 1898–1921*. Milwaukee: Bruce Publishing Company, 1955.

BIG EYES

Edited by Dana Asbury

Designed by Kristina E. Kachele

Typography in Bembo by

Keystone Typesetting, Inc.

Printed and bound by

Thomson-Shore, Incorporated

Jacket printed by Land O'Sun Printers